P9-AGV-037

The Psychology of Romantic Love

- What is the distinctive nature of romantic love?
- How can a loving relationship be a path to self-discovery?
- What is the difference between mature and immature love?
- What is the role of sex in romantic love?
- Does romantic love necessarily imply sexual exclusivity?
- How do we deal with jealousy?

Dr. Nathaniel Branden, bestselling author and distinguished psychologist and psychotherapist offers answers to these and many more questions about the most passionate of all human relationships.

"A wise, humane and helpful book."

—*Publishers Weekly*

"This is a bold, important book. *The Psychology of Romantic Love* will do more for lovers than all the sex manuals on the shelves."

—George Leonard, author of *The Ultimate Athlete*, past president of the Association for Humanistic Psychology

"The book is readable, informative and inspirational."

—Virginia Satir, author of *Peoplemaking*

"In *The Psychology of Romantic Love* Dr. Nathaniel Branden offers us a rare and potent gift. With the passion that comes from true knowing, he shows us how loving can become an evolutionary event, consummate in its capacity to deepen, unsurpassed in its power to transform."

—Jean Houston, Ph.D., Director of the Foundation for Mind Research

A PSYCHOLOGY TODAY BOOK CLUB
MAIN SELECTION

The Psychology of Romantic Love

•

What Love Is,
Why Love Is Born,
Why It Sometimes Grows,
Why It Sometimes Dies

•

Nathaniel Branden, Ph.D.

BANTAM BOOKS
TORONTO • NEW YORK • LONDON • SYDNEY • AUCKLAND

*This low-priced Bantam Book
has been completely reset in a type face
designed for easy reading, and was printed
from new plates. It contains the complete
text of the original hard-cover edition.*
NOT ONE WORD HAS BEEN OMITTED.

THE PSYCHOLOGY OF ROMANTIC LOVE
A Bantam Book

PRINTING HISTORY
*Tarcher edition published June 1980
5 printings through August 1980*
A Selection of Psychology Today Book Club March 1980
*Bantam edition / September 1981
2nd printing . . . April 1983*

Back cover photo by Glen Christiansen.

ISBN 0-553-23683-0

Published simultaneously in the United States and Canada

PRINTED IN THE UNITED STATES OF AMERICA

H   11 10 9 8 7 6 5 4

To Patrecia Wynand Branden

Acknowledgments

This is to acknowledge the invaluable assistance of Dr. Cheri Adrian, who assembled and organized over fifteen years of my miscellaneous lectures and writings on the subject of romantic love and who, in addition, made immensely helpful contributions to this work in the area of historical research.

I want also to acknowledge the contributions of Jonathan Hirschfeld in the area of historical research.

My thanks to Barbara Branden, who, along with Dr. Adrian and Mr. Hirschfeld, made many valuable editorial suggestions.

My appreciation and deeply felt regard for the sensitivity and skill of my publisher, Jeremy Tarcher, and his superlative editor, Janice Gallagher, whose contributions enhanced in so many ways the quality of this book.

And finally, my deepest gratitude to Devers Branden, who lived through the writing of this book with me on a daily basis, made many helpful suggestions, and provided the emotional support without which I am not certain this book could have been written.

Contents

Romantic love is for grown-ups; it is not for children. It is not for children in the literal sense, and also in the psychological sense: not for those who, regardless of age, still experience themselves as children.

Chapter Four: "The Challenges of Romantic Love"

Introduction

The passionate attraction between man and woman that is known as romantic love can generate the most profound ecstasy. It can also generate, when frustrated, the most unutterable suffering. Yet for all its intensity, the nature of that attachment is little understood. To some, who associate "romantic" with "irrational," romantic love is a temporary neurosis, an emotional storm, inevitably short-lived, which leaves disillusionment and disenchantment in its wake. To others, romantic love is an ideal that, if never reached, leaves one feeling one has somehow missed the secret of life.

Looking at the tragedy and confusion so many experience in romantic relationships, many persons have concluded that the idea of romantic love is somehow fundamentally wrong, a false hope. In consequence, more and more people are experimenting with different kinds of relationships, ones that do not entail the intimacy and vulnerability of an intense commitment to another person. Some people have given up the hope of any passionate attachment as not only false but pernicious. Romantic love is also under attack today from psychologists, sociologists, and anthropologists, who frequently scorn it as an immature, illusory ideal. To such intellectuals, the idea that an intense emotion-

I

al attachment could form the basis of a lasting, fulfilling relationship is simply a neurotic product of modern Western culture.

We have long been witness to the fact that many persons begin a relationship genuinely in love and with goodwill and high hopes for the future, and then, across time, tragically, painfully, and with a good deal of bewilderment, watch the relationship deteriorate and ultimately collapse. They think back to a time when they were deeply in love, when so much seemed right and good and rewarding, and they are tortured by not knowing how and why they lost what they had. If *that* love could die, they find themselves feeling, can *any* love last? Is romantic love possible for me at all? Or for anyone? Perhaps it's time to put the dream away along with the rest of the toys of childhood. And sometimes they reach a day when even these questions are forgotten, when the anguish of *why* and *how* has long since faded, and all that is left is numbness. Sometimes they console themselves with the belief that this numbness is what it means finally to grow up. And, in our culture, there are many persons who encourage them in this belief.

And yet . . . people continue to fall in love. The dream dies, only to be reborn, like a life force not to be stopped. The drama continues. Moved by a passion they do not understand toward a fulfillment they seldom reach, they are haunted by the vision of a distant possibility that refuses to be extinguished.

The vision refuses to be extinguished because it answers profound human needs. But what is the nature of those needs? What is the nature of that possibility that eternally inspires our imagination and ignites our longing? And what stands between us and the successful fulfillment of our longing? In the course of our journey, these are the questions we shall undertake to answer.

Let me state at the outset that I am writing from the conviction that romantic love is not a fantasy or an aberration but one of the great possibilities of our existence, one of the great adventures, and one of the great challenges. I am writing from the conviction that ecstasy is one of the normal factors of our emotional life, or can be.

I do not see romantic love as the prerogative of youth. Nor do I see it as some kind of immature ideal, inappropriately adapted from literature, that must crumble in the face of "practical reality." I do see romantic love as requiring more of us, in terms of our personal evolution and maturity, than we generally appreciate. Indeed, that is one of the central themes of this book.

There are different kinds of love that can unite one human being with another. Let me begin with a general definition of the category of love to be explored in this book. Romantic love is *a passionate spiritual-emotional-sexual attachment between a man and a woman that reflects a high regard for the value of each other's person.*

I do not describe a relationship as romantic love if the couple does not experience their attachment as passionate or intense, at least to some significant extent. I do not describe a relationship as romantic love if there is not some experience of spiritual affinity, some deep mutuality of values and outlook, some sense of being "soul mates"; if there is not deep emotional involvement; if there is not a strong sexual attraction. And if there is not mutual admiration—if, for example, there is mutual contempt instead—again I do not describe the relationship as romantic love.

Almost any statement we make about love, sex, or man/woman relationships entails something of a personal confession. We speak from what we have lived. When a psychologist undertakes to address the subject of love, he cannot avoid telling the world about himself. This does not mean that the issues involved are incorrigibly subjective and that no valid general observations can be made. I shall argue to the contrary. Our reflections are not the product solely of our own romantic history; but many of their roots do lie deep in that soil, and draw up, with or without our awareness, many of the feelings, values, and conclusions that we may offer as "obvious."

It would be self-deceiving for me to pretend that this book would be as it is if I had not had the experience of being passionately in love with a woman for fifteen years. Patrecia Wynand Branden died in a freak drowning accident on March 31, 1977. On the morning of that day we lingered in bed, making love and talking about the excitement we felt in each other's presence, an excitement like no other in our lives, that seemed almost magically and irresistibly self-rejuvenating. When Patrecia entered the room, the lights of my world got brighter—for fifteen years. It would be inappropriate for me to pretend that that experience does not affect the thoughts that go through my head when I hear colleagues speak of the "inevitability" of romantic love's dying within a few months (or weeks) of its gratification.

My personal context aside, this book draws upon two primary sources. First, the book represents an attempt to reason about and understand man/woman relationships on the basis of facts and data more or less available to everyone, the material of history and of culture. Second, the positions advanced are grounded in my experiences as a psychotherapist and marriage counselor. Having had the opportunity to work with thousands of people over the past twenty-five years and to see the nature of their struggle to achieve sexual and romantic fulfillment—and the ways in which they so often sabotage their own aspirations—I am left with a great many conclusions about what men and women consciously or subconsciously seek from one another, as well as conclusions about why there is so much failure, misery, and suffering in their relationships. More recently, I have been conducting three-and-a-half-day workshops throughout the country on *Self-Esteem and the Art of Being* and *Self-Esteem and Romantic Relationships,* and in these Intensives (as they are called) I have had many opportunities to explore further and test the ideas and conclusions that are put forth in this book.*

It is useful to remember that, throughout most of the past, the concept of romantic love as an ideal and as the expected basis for marriage was unknown; it is still unknown in many cultures of the world. Only during the past several decades have some of the educated classes in non-Western cultures rebelled against the tradition of marriage arranged by families and looked to the West and its concept of romantic love as a preferred ideal. While in Western Europe the idea of romantic love has had a long history, its acceptance as the proper basis of a long-term, established relationship such as marriage has never been as widespread as it has been in American culture.

In the course of this book, a concept of romantic love emerges that goes considerably beyond that associated with the American concept of love. But it is best understood historically in the context of the American ideal as contrasted with that of earlier cultures.

Young people growing up in twentieth-century North America take for granted certain assumptions about their future with the opposite sex, assumptions that are by no means shared by every other culture. These include that the two people who will share their lives will choose each other, freely and voluntarily, and that no one, neither family nor friends, church or state, can or should make that choice for them; that they will choose on the basis of love, rather than on the basis of social, family, or financial considerations; that it very much matters which human being they choose and, in this connection, that the differences between one human being and another are immensely important; that they can hope and expect to derive happiness from the relationship with the person of their choice and that the pursuit of such happiness is entirely normal, indeed

*Information about the Intensives may be obtained by writing to The Biocentric Institute, P.O. Box 1009, Beverly Hills, CA 90213.

is a human birthright; and that the person they choose to share their life with and the person they hope and expect to find sexual fulfillment with are one and the same.

Throughout most of human history, all of these views would have been regarded as extraordinary, even incredible.

And so in Chapter 1 I shall sketch the highlights of the process by which this view of love and man/woman relationships emerged and became prevalent in the Western world. The purpose of such an historical overview is to establish a context for where we are today, to see our struggles in perspective, and to become more conscious of attitudes and values from the past that are still operative within us to the detriment of our efforts to achieve happiness in relationships.

In order that these goals be accomplished, the historical overview encompasses themes that are philosophical, political, ethical, and literary, because all influence the way we think about and understand the nature and problems of romantic love today.

In Chapter 2 we shall shift from a *sociohistorical* to a *psychological* orientation—as we begin to develop an understanding of the roots and meaning of romantic love, not in the context of the past but of the present, the *timeless present,* in the context of our nature as human beings. We shall examine the basic psychological needs that generate the hunger for romantic love and that it aims at fulfilling. In so doing, we can begin to understand the sources of the rapture—or pain—of our love relationships.

In Chapter 3, we shall consider fundamental factors that influence who we are likely to fall in love with— the process of selection. At this point, we shall have explored the themes "what love is and why love is born."

In Chapter 4 we shall address the questions "why it sometimes grows, why it sometimes dies." We shall address ourselves to the issue of what romantic love requires of us—requires psychologically—if it is to succeed. We shall explore the *challenges* of romantic love. We shall describe basic determinants of fulfilment or defeat in this area, deepening our understanding of both our victories and our disappointments.

This book is neither a love manual nor a sex manual. While certain "how to" elements inevitably appear at key points, either explicitly or implicitly, advice giving is not the purpose of the book. The purpose is to make romantic love intelligible—to enrich our understanding of such love—and to celebrate the vision of romantic love as a realistic and worthwhile attainment for men and women of all ages.

ONE

•

The Evolution of Romantic Love

Prologue: Love and Defiance

Stories of passionate love relationships between men and women exist throughout our literature and are a treasured part of our cultural heritage. The great love affairs of Lancelot and Guinevere, Heloise and Abelard, Romeo and Juliet live for us as symbols of physical passion and spiritual devotion. But such stories are tragedies—and tragedies of a very revealing kind.

The lovers are impressive not because they typify their societies but because they rebel against them. The lovers are memorable because they are unusual. Their love challenges the moral and social codes of their culture, and their stories are tragic because the lovers are defeated by those codes.

Implicit in the tragic nature of these love stories, implicit in the fact that the lovers' commitment to each other represented a defiant no flung in the face of their culture or society, is the fact that such love was not regarded as a "normal" way of life or an accepted cultural ideal.

The ideal of romantic love stands in opposition to much of our history, as we shall see. First of all, it is individualistic. It rejects the view of human beings as

9

interchangeable units, and it attaches the highest importance to individual differences as well as to individual choice. Romantic love is egoistic, in the philosophical, not in the petty, sense—egoism as a philosophical doctrine holds that self-realization and personal happiness are the moral goals of life—and romantic love is motivated by the desire for personal happiness. Romantic love is secular. In its union of physical with spiritual pleasure in sex and love, as well as in its union of romance and daily life, romantic love is a passionate commitment to this earth and to the exalted happiness that life on earth can offer.

The definition of romantic love offered in the Introduction—*a passionate spiritual-emotional-sexual attachment between a man and a woman that reflects a high regard for the value of each other's person*—contains all of these elements, and their importance will become more and more apparent as we proceed. In particular we shall come to appreciate how intimately related are the themes of individualism and romantic love. In that same context we shall need to reappraise the issue of *selfishness,* to move beyond conventional ways of thinking and to recognize how indispensable to our life and well-being is rational intelligent or enlightened selfishness; an honest respect for self-interest is a necessity of survival and certainly of romantic love.

The music that inspires the souls of lovers exists within themselves and the private universe they occupy. They share it with each other; they do not share it with the tribe—or with society. The courage to hear that music and to honor it is one of the prerequisites of romantic love.

The Relevance of History: Recurring Themes

The evolution of man/woman relationships is part of the evolution of human consciousness. We carry the past within us—sometimes as an asset, sometimes as a liability—and we who live in the last third of the twentieth century cannot fully understand the conflicts and blocks within our own psyche which obstruct our efforts to achieve happiness in love relationships unless we are conscious of our history, of the steps by which we arrived where we are today.

When we look at the development of man/woman relationships across the centuries, we see motion, progress, retrogression, detours, and forward motion again —something like the path of evolution itself. The emergence of a rational concept of romantic love has required a long process of development.

The purpose of the brief review that follows is to help us understand the steps of that development and to isolate certain recurring themes that seem almost timeless in their persistence, in our past and in our present. In whatever time and culture we look, it is impossible for some of us not to encounter ourselves. Let us begin.

The Tribal Mentality: The Unimportance of the Individual

Economics, not love, was the motivating force for union in primitive societies—indeed, in virtually all hunting and agricultural societies. The family was a unit established for the purpose of optimizing the chances of physical survival. Man/woman relationships were conceived and defined not in terms of "love," or of psychological needs for "emotional intimacy," but in terms of the practical needs associated with hunting, fighting, raising crops, child-rearing, and so forth.*

So far as we can ascertain, in primitive cultures the idea of romantic love did not exist at all. The cardinal

---

*Since survival in a preindustrial society depended so crucially on physical strength and physical skills, the division of labor between man and woman was predominantly determined on the basis of their respective physical capacities. Man's superior physical strength, and woman's need of protection, especially during periods of pregnancy and child-bearing, were made a justification for the inequality of the sexes and woman's subordination to man.

and ruling value was the survival of the tribe. The individual was subordinated to the tribe's needs and rules in virtually every aspect of life. This was—is— the essence of "the tribal mentality." Little or no importance was granted to the worth of the individual personality and little or none to individual emotional attachments.

While these conclusions can only be inferences, they are well-supported by anthropological studies of primitive societies still in existence in our own century. As Morton M. Hunt (1960) writes:

> By and large, the clanship structure and social life of most primitive societies provides wholesale intimacy and a broad distribution of affection; . . . most primitive peoples fail to see any great difference between individuals, and hence do not become involved in unique connections in the Western fashion; any number of trained observers have commented on the ease of their detachment from love objects, and their candid belief in the interchangeability of loves. Dr. Audrey Richards, an anthropolgist who lived among the Bemba of Northern Rhodesia in the 1930s, once related to a group of them an English folk-fable about a young prince who climbed glass mountains, crossed chasms, and fought dragons, all to obtain the hand of a maiden he loved. The Bemba were plainly bewildered, but remained silent. Finally an old chief spoke up, voicing the feelings of all present in the simplest of questions: "Why not take another girl?" he asked.

Margaret Mead's well-known study of the Samoans (1949) shows likewise that deep emotional attachments between individuals are very foreign to such societies' psychology and pattern of living. While sexual promiscuity and a short duration of sexual relationships are sanctioned and encouraged, any tendency to form strong emotional bonds between individuals is actively discouraged.

In the mores regulating sexual activity in primitive cultures, one often encounters a fear of, even an antagonism toward, sexual attachments that grow out of (what we would call) love. Indeed, sexual activity often appears acceptable to most when the feelings that prompt it are superficial. "In the Trobriand islands, for instance," writes G. Rattray Taylor (1973):

> Adults do not mind if children engage in sexual play and attempt precociously to perform the sexual act; as adolescents, they may sleep with one another, provided only that they are not in love with one another. If they fall in love, the sexual act becomes forbidden, and for lovers to sleep together would outrage decency.

Love, if it occurs, is sometimes more severely regulated than sex. (Of course, in many instances there is not even a word for "love" in any sense approximating our own.) Passionate individual attachments are evidently seen as threatening to tribal values and tribal authority.

We need to note that the issue is not primitiveness as such, but the tribal mentality. One encounters it again in the technologically advanced society of George Orwell's *1984,* where the full power and authority of a totalitarian state is aimed at crushing the self-assertive individualism of romantic love. The contempt of twentieth century dictatorships for a citizen's desire to have "a personal life," the characterization of such a desire as "petty bourgeois selfishness," is too well-known to require documentation.

The tribal mentality, ancient or modern, tends to regard romantic love as socially subversive, as somehow threatening to the welfare of the tribe—that is, society.

The Greek Perspective: Spiritual Love

The concept of love as an important value and the idea of it as a passionate spiritual attachment, based on mutual admiration, between one human being and another, did exist and in fact was a matter for philosophical discussion in the culture of classical Greece. But this love was conceived as a very "special" attachment that had little to do with the actual relations between human beings and the ordinary conduct of their daily lives—and nothing to do with the institution of marriage.

Parenthetically—this point should be stressed at the outset—I do not wish to imply that sex is only justifiable in the context of love, or that love necessarily should eventuate in marriage. Obviously sex, love, and marriage are three separate and distinct, though in some contexts related, phenomena. I shall elaborate on my view of their relationship later. Here it is perhaps necessary to point out not that sex necessarily implies love but that romantic love necessarily implies sex, and not that love should necessarily entail marriage but that marriage should entail love. This acknowledged, let us continue.

Despite the fact that much of Greek culture reflects a worship of physical beauty, clearly evident in attitudes toward sex and love was the view that a person was made of two disparate elements: flesh, which pertained to one's "lower" nature, and spirit, which pertained to one's "higher." The needs and goals of the flesh were inferior to those of the spirit; what was exalted and most precious was that which was most remote from the body and its activities.

Closely related to the soul-body dichotomy was another division—that between reason and passion. "Reason" meant cool, uninvolved detachment, and "passion" was seen as necessarily representing a failure of reason.

The Greeks idolized the spiritual, not the carnal, relationship between lovers, and for the Greeks, this profound, spiritually significant love was possible only in the context of homosexual relationships, usually between older men and younger boys. Although there is some dispute concerning the prevalence of homosexuality in Greece, it was clearly much more prevalent than in our own culture and among many intellectuals came to be regarded as "the expression of the highest type of human emotion." (Hunt, 1960) While sexual desire apart from deeper feeling was often regarded as effeminate and unhealthy, a passionate love relationship between two men was idealized as a relationship in which the older lover inspired the younger to nobility and virtue, and the love between them elevated the mind and the emotions of both.

On the other hand, antifeminism was a pronounced theme in the culture of classical Greece, and although the Greeks were scarcely indifferent to heterosexual sex or to female beauty, they viewed their interest as being devoid of ethical meaning or spiritual significance. Both Plato and Aristotle agreed that women were inferior to men in body and in mind. Women were brought up to see themselves as subordinate to men in virtually every respect. They had very little status before the law; they required legal guardians; they shared almost none of the rights guaranteed to male Greek citizens. The practical economic functions that women had performed in earlier times were now largely performed by slaves. No longer men's partners in the struggle for survival, women had less importance in a man's world.

Were a man to fall in love with a woman, it was highly unlikely that the woman would be his wife. Far more likely, she would be a courtesan—a highly educated woman, trained to be mentally stimulating as well as sexually exciting, an intellectual as well as a sexual companion. But most Greeks looked with contempt upon a man who fell in love even with a courtesan.

Except in its ideal sense as an elevating admiration, which could exist only among men, "love" was predominately viewed as a pleasurable, enjoyable game, an amusement, a diversion, of no deep importance or lasting significance. Passionate sexual love, when it appeared, was commonly regarded as a tragic madness, an affliction that took possession of a man and carried him away from that calm, cool evenness of disposition so much admired by the Greeks.

The notion of "marrying for love" was consequently as absent from the thinking of the Greeks as it was from the thinking of primitive man. "Marriage," wrote the Greek poet Pallatas, "brings a man only two happy days: the day he takes his bride to bed and the day he lays her in her grave." A wife was expensive, a burden, often a hindrance to a man's freedom. But it was generally held that a man owed it to the state and to his religion to have children; he needed a housekeeper; and a new wife brought a dowry. Marriage was a necessary evil and a match between unequals.

The Roman Perspective: A Cynical View of Love

From the point of view of the dominant philosophy of Rome, Stoicism, passionate involvement was a threat to the pursuit of duty. The hero of Rome's epic, Aeneas, easily turns away from the passion of his lover Dido to pursue his duty of founding the Roman republic. Like the Greeks, Roman intellectuals looked upon passion as a kind of madness.

The Romans, like the Greeks, did not marry for love. Among the upper classes, marriages were usually arranged between families for financial or political reasons; and a man married to acquire a housekeeper and to have children.

Yet in Roman culture, the family took on a new significance as a political and social unit—chiefly for reasons having to do with the preservation and protection of property. Roman law, which carefully provided for the transfer of property from one generation to the next, came to include complex laws governing forms of marriage between different classes of Roman citizens as well as those of other peoples in the empire. The cultural and political importance of the family gave a new importance to the relationship between husbands and wives. Cultural mythology supported a religious devotion to the Roman family, extolling in particular the virtues of virginity in unmarried, and fidelity in married, women. Certain moralists—and even, at times, lawgivers—required fidelity even of husbands.

The increased valuation of the domestic unit was accompanied by an elevation in the position of women. Women in Rome gained significantly in legal status and enjoyed a far greater measure of freedom, economic independence, and cultural respect than they had known previously. They were more likely, then, to be in a position of equality in a love relationship. In this respect, they approached at least one of the conditions of romantic love—equality—since the relationship of a superior to an inferior, or a master to a subordinate, cannot qualify as romantic love.

Roman epitaphs, letters between husbands and wives, and occasional references by contemporary social observers evidence the strength of the marital bond and the existence of long, harmonious, even affectionate, unions between some partners. But passion remained very foreign to their view of marriage.

At the height of the Roman empire, and through the period of its disintegration, both men and women sought the experience of passion, the excitement and glamour of sexual relationships in extramarital adventures and affairs of the sort made famous by the poet Ovid's *Ars Amatoria*. At the height of the empire, adultery on the part of both sexes was widespread and virtually taken for granted as a sport necessary to relieve the tedium of existence; the aristocrats of Rome indulged in the jaded, frenetic sensuality that we associate with Roman decadence: a vicious mixture of love and hatred, attraction and revulsion, desire and hostility. The most famous Roman literature of romantic passion, Ovid's description of "the art of love" and Catullus's love poems to "Lesbia," portray lovers as immersed in sensuality, tormenting each other with infidelities and elaborate games of power. There is in particular a considerable literature of hostile complaint against the tyrannical sensuality of newly powerful women, as exhibited in Juvenal's Sixth Satire:

> A wife is a tyrant—the more so if her husband is fond or loving. Cruelty is natural to women: they torment their husbands, whip the housekeeper, and enjoy having slaves flogged almost to death. Their sexual lusts are disgusting—they prefer slaves, actors, and gladiators; their efforts to sing and play musical instruments are a bore; and their gluttonous eating and drinking are enough to make a man sick.

Thus, the same culture that generated the first ideal of domestic felicity and mutual respect among men and women, the same culture that institutionalized elaborate forms of marriage, was a culture in which sex and love, passion and caring interpersonal relationships, appear as polar opposites. The union of sex with love, so basic to our modern concept of romantic love, was viewed cynically, if recognized at all.

The Message of Christianity: Nonsexual Love

In the second and third centuries, during the growing decadence of the Roman empire, a new cultural and historical force began to make its impact felt on the Western world, a force that would affect man/woman relationships as profoundly as it affected the rest of Western culture: Christianity. The central thrust of this new religion was a profound asceticism, an intense hostility to human sexuality, and a fanatical scorn of earthly life. Hostility to pleasure—above all, to sexual pleasure—was not merely one tenet among many of this new religion; it was central and basic. The Church's hostility to sex was rooted in its hostility to physical—earthly—existence and its view that physical enjoyment of life on earth necessarily meant spiritual evil. While such doctrines were already present in the Roman world in the doctrines of Stoicism, Neoplatonism, and Oriental mysticism, Christianity mobilized the sentiments behind such doctrines, capitalizing on the growing revulsion against the mindless decadence of the time and offering the appeal of a cleansing and purifying acid.

Saint Paul elevated the Greek concept of the soul-body dichotomy to unprecedented importance in the Western world. The soul, he taught, is an entity separate from the body, transcending the latter, and its proper sphere of concern is with values unrelated to the body or to this earth. The body is only a prison in which the soul is trapped. It is the body that drags a person down to sin, to the quest for pleasure, to sexual lust.

Christianity upheld to men and women an ideal of love that was consistently selfless and nonsexual. Love and sex were, in effect, proclaimed to stand at opposite poles: the source of love was God; the source of sex was, in effect, the devil.

"It is good for a man not to touch a woman," taught Saint Paul; but if men lack the necessary self-control "let them marry: for it is better to marry than to burn [with lust]."

Sexual abstinence was proclaimed the moral ideal. Marriage—later described as a "medicine for immorality"—was Christianity's reluctant concession to the depravity of human nature that made this ideal actually obtainable. Taylor (1973) writes:

> The Medieval Church was obsessed with sex to a quite painful degree. Sexual issues dominated its thinking in a manner which we should regard as entirely pathological. It is hardly too much to say that the ideal which it held out to Christians was primarily a sexual ideal.
>
> This ideal was a highly consistent one and was embodied in a most elaborate code of regulations. The Christian code was based, quite simply, on the conviction that the sexual act was to be avoided like the plague, except for the bare minimum necessary to keep the race in existence. Even when performed for this purpose it remained a

regrettable necessity. Those who could were ex-
horted to avoid it entirely, even if married. For
those incapable of such heroic self-denial there
was a great spider's web of regulations whose
overriding purpose was to make the sexual act as
joyless as possible and to restrict its performance
to the minimum—that is, to restrict it exclusively
to the function of procreation. It was not actually
the sexual act which was damnable, but the pleasure derived from it—and this pleasure remained
damnable even when the act was performed for
the purpose of procreation. . . .

Not only the pleasure of the sexual act was
held sinful, but also the sensation of desire for a
person of the opposite sex, even when unconsummated. Since the love of a man for a woman was
held to be simply desire, this led to the incon-
trovertible proposition that no man should love
his wife. In fact, Peter Lombard maintained . . .
that for a man to love his wife too ardently is a
sin worse than adultery . . .

Apart from its role as a "medicine for immorality,"
marriage during the Middle Ages was still regarded
essentially as an economic and political institution,
although declared by the Church to be a sacrament. By
the end of the sixth century, the Church had adopted
political authority over marriage as it had assumed
authority over other aspects of secular life. The severe
regulation of man/woman relationships by Church
power extended from start to finish. The Church re-
placed its authority for that of parental consent as the
arranger and sanctioner of marriage, and it banned
divorce and remarriage without papal dispensation.

What is rarely appreciated today, and what is particularly interesting to note in the Church's attitude,
was that the integration of love and sex was regarded
not as a noble ideal but as a vice:

For in the eyes of the Church, for a priest to
marry was a worse crime than to keep a mistress,

and to keep a mistress was worse than to engage in random fornication—a judgment which completely reverses secular conceptions of morality, which attach importance to the quality and durability of personal relationships. When accused of being married, it was always a good defense to reply that one was simply engaged in indiscriminate seduction, for this carried only a light penalty, while the former might involve total suspension. (Taylor, 1973)

It was not a great sin, in the eyes of the medieval church, for a priest to fornicate with a whore. But for a priest to fall in love and marry, that is, for his sex life to be integrated as an expression of his total person, was a cardinal offense.

It is significant that the Church's most ferocious wrath was reserved not for fornication but for masturbation. It is through masturbation that a human being first discovers the sensual potential of his or her own body; moreover, it is an entirely "selfish" act, in that it is performed solely for the benefit of the person involved. It is the act through which many an individual first encounters the possibility of an ecstasy entirely different from the ecstasy promised by religion.

The Church's essential antisexualism was paralleled by an essential antifeminism. With the rise of Christianity in medieval Europe, women lost virtually all the rights they had won under the Romans; they were regarded, in effect, as vassals of the male, to whom they were to be entirely subordinate; more precisely, they were regarded as domesticated animals. There were disputes as to whether or not women possessed souls. The proper relationship of woman to man, according to Christian doctrine, is that of man's relationship to God: just as man is to accept God as his master and submit himself unquestioningly to God's will, so must woman recognize man as her master and submit herself unquestioningly to his will. That woman should be entirely subordinate to man was justified, in part, on the ground that Eve had been the cause of Adam's downfall and therefore the cause of all the suffering men had to endure thereafter.

Later in the Middle Ages, a second view of woman emerged and coexisted with the first. On the one hand, woman was symbolized by Eve, the sexual temptress, the cause of man's spiritual downfall. On the other hand, she existed in the image of Mary, the Virgin Mother, the symbol of purity who transforms and lifts man's soul upward. The whore and the virgin—or the whore and the mother—have dominated the concept of woman in Western culture ever since.

To state the dichotomy in modern terms: There is the woman one desires and the woman one admires; there is the woman one sleeps with and the woman one marries.

In its attitude toward woman, too, Christianity exhibited profound antagonism to a love relationship that integrates desire and admiration, physical and spiritual values, and which is based on the essential equality of the partners. On the deepest level Christianity has always been a fierce opponent of romantic love.

The pursuit of one's values, the exercise of one's judgment in the conduct of one's life, and the enjoyment of sexual pleasure—all are acts of *self*-assertion entailed in the choice and experience of a romantic relationship. All were condemned by Christianity.

Courtly Love: A Primitive Foreshadowing of Romantic Love

Given the brutally inhuman sexual repressiveness of the Middle Ages and the strict regulation of marriage by the church, it is not astonishing that the first blind groping toward a better view of the man/woman relationship should emerge in the form of a strange concoction of beliefs about love and marriage known as the "doctrine of courtly love." Originating in the south of France in the eleventh century, the doctrine of courtly love was developed by troubadours and poets in the courts of the nobility—courts often ruled by the wives of nobles gone off to the Crusades.

The doctrine upheld as an ideal an exalted passion between a man and a woman; not between a man and his wife, but between a man and someone else's wife. Love, this time in a passionate and spiritual sense, was identified specifically with extramarital involvements. Courtly love thus maintained the dismal view of marriage that had been accepted for hundreds of years. There is considerable controversy over the extent to which courtly love was an actual, or mainly a literary, phenomenon, but the fact that it is recorded signifies that it was a concept in the medieval mind.

A "code of love" proclaimed by the countess of Champagne in 1174 expresses in literary form the various tenets of courtly love: 1. Marriage is no good excuse against loving [that is, loving someone other than one's spouse]. . . . 3. No one can bind himself to two loves at once. . . . 8. No one, without abundant reason, ought to be deprived of his own love. 9. No one can love unless urged thereto by the hope of being loved. . . . 13. Love that is known publicly rarely lasts. 14. An easy conquest renders love despised, a difficult one makes it desired. . . . 17. A new love makes one quit the old. . . . 19. If love lessens, it dies speedily and rarely regains health. 20. The man prone to love is always prone to fear. 21. Real jealousy always increases the worth of love. 22. Suspicion and the jealousy it kindles increases love's worth. . . . 25. The true lover thinks naught good but what he believes pleases the co-lover. 26. Love can deny love nothing. . . . 28. The least presumption compels the lover to suspect evil of the co-lover. . . . (Langdon-Davies, 1927)

This famous code then declares:

> We pronounce and decree by the tenour of these presents, that love cannot extend its powers over two married persons; for lovers must grant everything, mutually and gratuitously the one to the other without being constrained thereunto by any motive of necessity; while husband and wife are

bound by duty to agree the one with the other and deny each other nothing. Let this judgment, which we have passed with extreme caution and with the advice of a great number of other ladies, be held by you as the truth, unquestionable and unalterable (ibid.)

Despite its many naivetés, contained within the doctrine of courtly love as an expressed ideal are three principles relative to the concept of romantic love as we understand it today: Authentic love between a man and a woman rests on and requires the free choice of each and cannot flourish in the context of submission to family or social or religious authority; such love is based on admiration and mutual regard; and love is not an idle diversion but is of great importance to one's life. In these respects, historians are justified in regarding the doctrine of courtly love as marking the beginning of the modern concept of romantic love.

But courtly love falls far below any mature understanding of romantic love, not only due to the magnitude of its psychological unrealism, which has been barely indicated here, but by its utter failure to integrate love and sex in any concrete manner. Courtly love was idealized to the extent that it remained unconsummated. The value of the love relationship was justified by the ennoblement of the lover, who was motivated to perform virtuous and courageous acts to win the love of his ideal; for the woman, it was justified by the fact that she was the source of such ennoblement. Unfulfilled and unsatisfied desire fueled the striving and the passion; few relationships were portrayed as surviving consummation. The affairs of the most famous of the courtly lovers, Lancelot and Guinevere, and Tristan and Isolde, ended in consummation—and in guilt and despair.* This was not a vision of love appropriate to men and women who wish to live on earth.

---

*Literature that presented consummated relationships was condemned by the church.

From the Renaissance to the Enlightenment: The Secularization of Love

In the political, economic, social, and cultural upheavals that characterized the Renaissance, the evolution toward the formulation of a joyful concept of man/woman love relationships continued, but without ever fundamentally challenging the underlying antisexualism and antifeminism that permeated Western culture. The fundamental guilt associated with the act of sex remained unabated. The soul-body dichotomy remained unchallenged.

Church authority as well as church power was lessened with the rise of Protestantism, and marriage was increasingly regarded as a necessary institution. Certainly, celibacy was still held to be preferable to carnal marriage even by the Reformation church, whose spokesmen maintained an unremitting hatred of human sexuality. Under the rule of Calvin, fornication was cause for exile and adultery cause for death by drowning or beheading.

The purpose of marriage was the production of offspring and "the remedying of incontinence." Sex was regarded as sinful but unrepressible, and Luther maintained that in marriage "God covers the sin."

Yet from the Renaissance onward, culture was increasingly secular. The rise of commerce and the development of an emerging middle class was accompanied by a new awakening to the possibilities and values of earthly existence. Religious antagonism to the possibilities of secular life was slowly and subtly being undermined. There was growing respect for marriage as an important institution in its own right and as a rewarding interpersonal relationship. The intellectuals of the fifteenth, sixteenth, and seventeenth centuries maintained that marriage ought to be arranged by families on the basis of "rational grounds," by which they meant grounds, "other than the self-interest of the participants." (Hunt, 1960) In this respect, the tradition of the past was continuing with the sole change, perhaps, that it was more fashionable to justify in the name of "reason."

However, in much of the literature of the period, predominantly in Shakespeare's plays, love was advocated as an important precondition to marriage. A few writers, such as Heinrich Cornelius Agrippa, went so far as to suggest that "love be the cause of marriage not substance of goodes;" that a man should "choose a wyfe, not a garment, let the wyfe be marryed not her dowrye." (ibid.) Among the most passionate and radical published opinions on man/woman relationships were those of John Milton, who argued that divorce should be allowed on grounds of "indisposition, unfitness, or contrariety of mind, arising from a cause in nature unchangeable, hindering and ever likely to hinder the main benefits of conjugal society, which are solace and peace." (ibid.) (Note: solace and peace, not excitement, not rapture, not ecstasy.)

There was, then, a growing effort to find a way of integrating love and marriage, to create a framework in which the expression of human sexuality would be acceptable, and in which feelings of love, tenderness, and affection could coexist with feelings of desire. But despite this new emphasis, the Puritan culture that succeeded Catholicism in dominating many Western countries remained, at core, antiromantic in its disparagement of earthly values and harshly repressive in its regulation of sexual behavior.

The later seventeenth and the eighteenth centuries witnessed among the educated classes an extreme reaction against Puritanism and, in general, an intense hostility toward church power in society and politics. But insofar as man/woman relationships were concerned, the "rebellion" amounted to an unrecognized capitulation. In "defiance" of religion, the writers and thinkers of what came to be called the Age of Reason tended to view a human being not as a sinner but, in effect, as a charming animal, feeble perhaps, but not depraved (in the religious sense)—and to view sex as a sport, an adventure, as devoid of spiritual meaning or significance as the cavorting of two animals.

The Age of Reason spawned such notions as that of "reasoned perversity," championed by such writers as Diderot and the Marquis de Sade, who in turn were to influence many of the Romantic writers of the nineteenth century. This trend, in "defying" religious morality, celebrated sexual cruelty. "Diderot, in fact, is one of the greatest exponents of that *Système de la Nature* which, carrying materialism to its logical consequences and proclaiming the supreme right of the individual to happiness and pleasure in opposition to the despotism of morality and religion, paves the way to the justification, in the name of Nature, of sexual perversions." (Praz, 1951)

The view of human beings which arose in this period cannot fully be understood without reference to the mechanistic vision of reality which had been given to the world by the new science. In a Newtonian universe of purely physical cause and effect, ultimately reducible to the blind motion of particles in space, the human spirit, not to mention the basic phenomenon of life itself, could only be viewed as fundamentally meaningless. Intellectuals influenced by this new world view and attempting to interpret human behavior developed their theories on mechanist-determinist premises, seeking the causes of behavior in humanity's primitive animal origins or the individual's role in the web of social forces; they sought to reduce the apparent complexity of human desires and purposes to rigid physical laws. From this point of view, the concept of a passionate spiritual relationship between a man and a woman seemed foolishly "unscientific," a deluded attempt to ennoble a purely physical impulse toward coupling.

In this Age of Reason, the dichotomy between reason and passion was resurrected in full force. The hallmark of the intellectual was contempt for emotions. Love, wrote Jonathan Swift (Hunt, 1960), is a "ridiculous passion which hath no being but in play-books and romances." For Sebastien Chamfort (ibid.), love was nothing but "the contact of two epidermises."

In rebellion against the alleged exalted values of religion which led to repression, people turned against the concept of exalted values in earthly human relationships—and did so, tragically, in the name of reason. Intellectuals of the period did not challenge religion's monopoly on exaltation and ecstasy; they merely surrendered exaltation and ecstasy.

But like previous cultures that assumed an inescapable conflict between reason and emotion, between spiritual-intellectual values and passionate-physical experience, the culture of the Age of Reason found itself obsessed with the passions it tried to discount. The culture, Hunt (1960) writes,

> Despite its contempt for emotion and its insistence that man's intellect should govern his actions, was obsessed with love, or rather with that special variant of it called "gallantry"—a socially required, intricate, ritualistic routine of flirtation, seduction and adultery.... The very men and women who spoke most nobly of subordinating their reason were helplessly addicted to squandering their time and money in amorous intrigues and ruining their health in excesses of lechery.

Love was a game, an amusement. Seduction and adultery were entertainment. Women were to be flattered, fooled, manipulated, toyed with, seduced, but never taken seriously. Lord Chesterfield (ibid.) wrote to his son, "Women are only children of a larger growth. They have an entertaining tattle and sometimes wit, but for solid reason and good sense, I never in my life knew one that had it."

It is worth noting that romantic love could not possibly coexist with such antifeminism. If the object of a man's passion is not to be taken seriously, the passion itself can hardly be viewed as having grandeur.

In the culture of England and Europe of this period,

then, marriage could hardly be based on love, as a general rule. Without doubt, exceptions did exist—and always have existed, through the ages. But we are dealing here, as throughout, with dominant and prevailing cultural trends.

Since the Renaissance, an increasing sympathy for the concept of secular happiness had been reflected in the idea that couples might grow to love each other *after* they were married. The idea of the legitimacy of marital happiness *at some level* was beginning to take hold. But marriage predominantly was still arranged by families for economic or political reasons, that is, for reasons of money and/or security and/or power.

In the realm of man/woman relationships, then, the thinkers of the Enlightenment advanced no ideas significantly different from, or superior to, those of their predecessors. In accepting the centuries-old division of a person into conflicting halves of body and spirit, they assured that physical passion and spiritual valuing would likewise remain unintegrated in relationships between men and women.

Industrialism, Capitalism, and a New Vision of Man/Woman Relationships

Yet in other areas of thought, notably in science and in political philosophy, reason was making unprecedented and spectacular advances.

This was a period of explosively rapid discovery in one field of intellectual investigation after another. In science, thinkers were proclaiming the power of the "unaided" mind to unlock the secrets of nature, to bring illumination to a world kept dark for centuries by a church-enforced blackout. And in politics, in the face of centuries of one form of tyranny after another, philosophers were discovering the Rights of Man. Both of these developments were to have a profound effect, in the nineteenth and twentieth centuries, on man/woman relationships.

The concept of romantic love as a widely accepted

cultural value and as the ideal basis of marriage was a product of the nineteeth century. It arose in the context of a culture that was predominantly secular and individualistic, a culture that explicitly valued life on earth and valued and recognized the importance of individual happiness. Such a culture was born in the Western world—most notably in the United States—with the birth of the Industrial Revolution and capitalism.

We cannot understand how romantic love arose as a cultural ideal if we do not understand the wider politicoeconomic context—which was to radically transform human beings' sense of the possibilities of life on earth.

With the Enlightenment, the Industrial Revolution, and the rise of capitalism in the nineteenth century— with the collapse of the absolute state and the development of a free-market society—human beings witnessed the sudden release of productive energy that previously had no outlet. They saw life made possible for countless millions who could have had no chance at survival in precapitalist economies. They saw mortality rates fall and population growth-rates explode upward. They saw themselves lifted to a standard of living no feudal baron could have conceived. With the rapid development of science, technology, and industry, people saw, for the first time in history, the liberated human mind taking control of material existence.

But industrialism and capitalism resulted in far more than an explosion of material well-being. For the first time in human history it was explicitly recognized that human beings *should be free to choose their own commitments*. Intellectual freedom and economic freedom rose and flourished together. Human beings had discovered the concept of individual *rights*.

Individualism was the creative power revolutionizing the world—and revolutionizing human relationships.

It was the United States, with its system of limited, constitutional government, that implemented the principle of capitalism—of free trade on a free market—to the greatest extent. In America, during the nineteenth century, the productive activities of human beings were *predominantly* left free of governmental regulations, controls, and restrictions. In the brief period of a century and a half, the United States created a level of freedom, of progress, of achievement, of wealth, of physical comfort—a standard of living—unmatched and unequaled by the total sum of humankind's development up to that time. *The United States created a context in which the pursuit of happiness on earth seemed natural and normal and possible.*

No less an opponent of capitalism than Friedrich Engels attributes the cultural elevation of chosen love relationships to the rise of industrialism and the free market:

> [Capitalism] dissolved all traditional relations, and for inherited customs and historical rights it substituted . . . "free" contract. . . .
>
> But contracts can only be concluded by people who can freely dispose of their person, actions and possessions, and who meet each other on equal terms.
>
> ....
>
> [Under capitalism] in moral theory as in poetry, nothing was more unshakably established than that every marriage not based on mutual sex love and on the really free agreement of man and wife, was immoral. In short, love-marriage was proclaimed a human right: not only as "droit de l'homme" but also, strange to say, as "droit de la femme."

In the area of man/woman relationships, this new development was felt most powerfully, perhaps, by women, as the quotation from Engels suggests. Social recognition of the equality of the sexes is historically rooted in that politicoeconomic system Engels so much despised. As we have seen, prior to the birth of capitalism, the family was, for most people, primarily a unit of economic survival. And since most people lived on the land, and since the larger the family, the more potential workers, woman's role as child-bearer was of central and primary importance. Her economic survival depended on this function and, more generally, on her relation to a man.

But in an industrial society, and with the emergence of cities, intellectual rather than physical skills assumed paramount importance. Physical strength as such is of comparatively little survival value in a machine civilization. Slowly, and against a resistance whose origins were predominantly traditional and religious, not political or economic, new possibilities of self-support became available to women.*

The economic independence of women, growing through the nineteenth and into the twentieth centuries, led irresistibly to social and legal independence, creating the possibility for man/woman relationships to be, to an unprecedented extent, relationships between equals.

The antifeminism and antisexualism spawned by religion had far from vanished in the nineteenth century; their influence, though diminishing, would reach deep into the twentieth. Indeed, the battle has not ended yet. But their demise has been inevitable since the development of industrialism, capitalism, and the philosophy of individualism. Antisexualism and antifeminism today are an historical anachronism.

From the beginnings of the Industrial Revolution, many social critics complained that capitalism had destroyed the social fabric of feudal relationships as well as the institution of family life. They warned that the independence men and women were winning under capitalism would lead to the end of civilization. They were correct to this extent: A new civilization, radically different from any that had been known before, was in the process of being born; and one of its characteris-

---

*It is unfortunate that today many advocates of women's rights mistakenly regard capitalism as their enemy; the historical truth is that it was capitalism that made it possible for a woman to earn an independent living. It was capitalism, with its underlying philosophy of individualism, that made the emergence of contemporary feminism historically inevitable.

tics was that men and women would choose to share their lives, not on the basis of economic necessity, but on the basis of their expectation of finding happiness and emotional fulfillment with one another.

The Impact of Romantic Literature

The beginnings of the Industrial Revolution coincided with another revolution that was to have an effect on man/woman relationships. This was the Romantic movement in literature.

The Romantic movement of the late eighteenth and early nineteenth centuries championed a perspective on human life which was to change Western culture in fundamental ways. First, Romanticism was individualistic: It regarded the individual person as an end in him- or herself and as a free agent in the choice of a life path. Second, Romanticism was profoundly value oriented: It regarded human life as governed not primarily by external forces—society or some metaphysical power—or by some internal "tragic flaw"—but rather by personally chosen values held by individual human beings. Indeed, the essence of Romanticism was its celebration of the passionately personal and individualistic.

As a literary school, Romanticism was an expression of the rising tide of individualism. At the base of this new movement was the concept of men and women as beings motivated by their *chosen* values. *Values* were seen as the crucial and determining element in human life.

Where courtly love had been highly formalized, conventionalized, and ritualized, the nineteenth-century Romantics celebrated idiosyncrasy and the "naturalness" of passion. Their vision of love was that of a desire for union between two highly individualistic souls who had a fundamental spiritual likeness, so that finding one's "soul mate," choosing the appropriate person, was of the highest importance.

For the first time, women began to appear in such

relationships—albeit rarely—as equal to men in intellect and in passion. Mary Wollstonecraft's *Vindication of the Rights of Women,* written in 1792, insisted in particular upon the rationality and intellectual ability of women. When Byron's romantic hero Manfred describes the woman he loved, he tells us that she had the same great capacities as his own: "She had the same lone thoughts and wanderings/The quest of hidden knowledge, and a mind/To comprehend the universe . . ."

Though this view of woman was certainly not the prevailing view (Romantic literature is filled with heroes and heroines who are perverse, cruel, melancholy, languishing, and sometimes sadomasochistic), it is clear that for the Romantics, the ideal relationship was one between beings of equal (if not identical) capacity and worth.

The necessity of freedom in their choice of partner was most loudly proclaimed by radicals like the British poet Shelley, who insisted that "love is free" and argued against marriage as a socioeconomic institution that inhibited emotional freedom. Known for their socially outrageous behavior, culture hero-villains like Lord Byron proclaimed their romantic capacity in numerous passionate affairs and flaunted even restrictions against incest—again stressing the importance of a free choice of lover. The important issue in sexual relationships was not whether sexual passion was legally sanctioned, but whether it arose from mutual love.

It is customary to understand the impact of literary Romanticism on man/woman relationships in terms of the love stories portrayed in Romantic novels, plays, and poems. But this perspective—if it is our exclusive focus—neglects what I believe to be a more fundamental source of Romanticism's influence. It is in the implicit *metaphysics* of Romanticism, that is, its view of the nature of life, the world, human nature, and the possibilities of human existence, that we can find the deepest explanation of its impact on culture and on cultural ideals and expectations.

Prior to the birth of the Romantic movement, the literature of Western civilization was dominated by the "fate" motif. Men and women were presented as the playthings—sometimes the defiantly rebellious, sometimes the sadly resigned, but almost always the defeated playthings—of an inexorable fate beyond their control, which determined the ultimate course of their life, regardless of their choices, wishes, or actions. In one form or another, the plays, epic poems, sagas, and chronicles that preceded the rise of Romantic literature carried the same message: Men and women are the pawns of destiny, caught in a universe essentially antagonistic to their interests, and if they ever do succeed, it is not by their own efforts, but by fortuitous external circumstances. This was a view of life against which Romanticism was rebelling.

In the Romantic plot-novel, on the other hand, the course of the characters' lives is determined by their chosen purpose, which they pursue through a series of relevant problems that must be solved, obstacles that must be overcome, conflicts that the characters must resolve—conflicts among the characters' values and/or conflicts with the values and purposes of others—through a series of coherent, integrated events leading to the climax of a final resolution. The philosophical implication is of course that our life is in our own hands, that our destiny is ours to shape, and that *choice* is the supreme fact of our existence. *This* is the deepest point of contact between Romanticism in literature and romantic love in the modern sense.

Unfortunately, the writers who sought to dramatize this view of the human situation were caught in a trap: They found, consciously or subconsciously, that the values of traditional morality were not applicable to this earth, could not be practiced, could not be lived successfully, could not serve as a human being's guide to success or happiness. This is the reason so many Romantic novels, whose sense of life is essentially pro-man/woman and pro-earth, have tragic endings, such as in Victor Hugo's *Notre Dame de Paris* or *The*

Man Who Laughs. This is also the reason so many Romantic novels are laid in the past, in some remote period of history—with a marked preference for the medieval era—such as the novels of Walter Scott, or the "costume" novels of today, which are among the last remnants of the Romantic school. A novel dealing with the crucial problems of the author's time, such as Hugo's *Les Misérables,* is a rare exception. By escaping from the problems of the present, the Romanticists contradicted their own (implicit) basic philosophical belief in human efficacy: They saw the individual as (sometimes) heroic, but life as (almost always) tragic. They could not successfully project and concretize the individual's fulfillment on earth; neither the traditional values of religion nor their own defiantly subjective (and often flagrantly irrational) values could make such fulfillment possible.

Taking flight into the historical past, or else taking refuge in novels of impossibly unrealistic sentimentality, the Romantic writers progressively became more vulnerable to the charge of "escapism" that was being raised against their work. They found themselves forced to retreat further and further from the actual problems of human existence, and, ultimately, to abandon all serious issues and concerns; their work degenerated into the class of light fiction, which is its predominant status today. (It is very common for opponents of the ideal of romantic love to charge it with the same failure of realism associated with Romanticism in literature.)

The Romanticists' view of life came under attack increasingly in the second half of the nineteenth century not only because their perspective was totally out of keeping with the mechanist-determinist-materialist world view of the period, which, in essence, saw human beings as helpless pawns of forces outside their control; and not only because of the infatuation with irrationalism and mysticism which permeated so much of the movement; and not only because too many of its exponents were unable to emancipate themselves from the undermining value orientation of religion; but, more fundamentally, because the Romanticists failed to grasp the importance of *reason* to their cause.

Accepting the reason-emotion dichotomy of their enemies, they proclaimed themselves champions of feeling against intellect, of subjectivity against objectivity. They did not grasp that reason and passion, or intellect and intuition, are equally expressions of our humanness and of the life force and need not be at war. They conceded reason to their enemies—a fatal error. The battle of the Romanticists against their enemies was not, in fact, a battle of irrationalists against rationalists, but rather of irrationalists (in some respects) against irrationalists (in some respects). Neither camp emerged as victor.

We have seen that what makes the term "romantic" applicable to both the Romantic plot-novel and the concept of romantic love is the vision of a human being's chosen values as the crucial determining element in his or her life. But what romantic love requires, and what the Romantic vision of the nineteenth century utterly failed to provide, is an *integration* of reason and passion—a balance between the subjective and the objective that human beings can live with. To express the same thought differently: What romantic love requires, and what Romantic writers fail to provide, is *psychological realism*.

The Nineteenth Century: "Tamed" Romantic Love

Notwithstanding the attacks on nineteenth-century Romanticism, the ideal of romantic love (in the most general sense of this term) spoke to the imagination of a middle class emerging in a time when the old philosophical and scientific, as well as social, certainties were breaking apart. It was in the mid-nineteenth century that the implications of the scientific world view came fully to awareness; evolution was only one in a long line of scientific discoveries undercutting the religious faiths that had for so long given significance and purpose to human existence. Commitment to interpersonal human relationships seemed the only source of stability, permanence, and meaning in human experience.

The last lines of Matthew Arnold's 1867 poem "Dover Beach" poignantly voice the extent to which love seemed the last stronghold of security:

> The Sea of Faith
> Was once ... at the full, and round earth's shore
> Lay like the folds of a bright girdle furled.
> But now I only hear
> Its melancholy, long, withdrawing roar,
> Retreating, to the breath
> Of the night-wind, down the vast edges drear
> And naked shingles of the world.
>
> Ah, love, let us be true
> To one another! for the world, which seems
> To lie before us like a land of dreams,
> So various, so beautiful, so new,
> Hath really neither joy, nor love, nor light,
> Nor certitude, nor peace, nor help for pain;
> And we are here as on a darkling plain
> Swept with confused alarms of struggle and flight,
> Where ignorant armies clash by night.

Love, then, was seen by many in the nineteenth century as a single point of security and support in a chaotic and unpredictable world, the one value to which men and women could cling with some hope of permanence.

It was among the middle classes in the nineteenth century that romantic love—in a "tamed" and domesticated sense—came to be regarded as an appropriate concomitant of marriage. Amid extensive upheaval, amid the rapid social and cultural changes that political freedom unleashed, marriage and family were idealized as institutions necessary for social stability, and conjugal devotion became, in effect, a social duty. This was not a very "romantic" view of romantic love. And because their morality was basically Puritan and their aspiration, as *nouveaux riches,* was for respectability, they domesticated and sentimentalized romantic passion—upholding the right to choose one's partner freely, but otherwise taming romantic love.

Victorian culture is known as a severely repressed one—at its worst, characterized in the romantic realm by a maudlin attitude toward the felicity of home and family life combined with a strict suppression of sexuality. Sexual desire, in this fundamentally Puritan society, tended to be regarded as a bestial passion of the male. In marriage, a man's bestial nature could be morally elevated by a virtuous, spiritual, sexless creature popularized in one influential novel as "the angel in the house." Victorian love combined mutual respect and devotion and affection with marriage, but greatly inhibited sex.

While freedom and individualism—the hallmarks of romantic love—were accepted values in the economic realm, the pressure of social conformity in the personal realm was enormous. Among the middle classes in particular, with their craving for "respectability," there was little of the emotional openness and freedom of sexual expression that are so basic to twentieth-century understanding of romantic love.

And yet, something had been unleashed that was not to be stopped. Irresistible changes were occurring. The position of women continued to improve as they won increasing rights with regard to property. Marriage became less a religious and more a civil commitment, and divorce became increasingly possible—legal changes that greatly facilitated the choice of romantic partners.

Finally, in the late nineteenth and early twentieth centuries, a new psychology was laying the foundations for a new understanding of sexuality—liberating sex, at least in some respects, from the religious view of its "bestiality" and replacing it with a view of sex as a natural function with profound psychological significance.

The impact of "the Freudian revolution," however, was paradoxical. While leading to a more enlightened perspective on human sexuality, it was, in its own way, deeply antiromantic and oppressive of women. Freud's antiromanticism did not consist of denying the right of individuals to choose their mates. He was not arguing for a return to arranged marriages. He merely declared that "love" was *really* "aim-inhibited sexuality," that bourgeois romanticism represented nothing more than an "over-idealization" of the lover resulting from a frustration of sexual longing. In Freud's view, "romantic love" is only a sublimated expression of darker sexual impulses. The concept of sexual desire as an expression of admiration was entirely foreign to his view of man/woman relationships, and, presumably, to his personal experience.

In his view of women, he totally subscribed to the doctrine of "the little woman," the fragile, not-too-bright creature who needs to be protected by the male from the harsh realities of existence. A woman's whole life, he taught, is marked by the sense of inadequacy she feels in consequence of not having a penis. Thus, a woman who is too active in the exercise of her intelligence, or otherwise ambitious in any worldly sense, is seen as engaging in an overcompensatory effort to deny her basic flawed and incomplete nature. Freud is not a hero to contemporary feminists.

And yet, in opening up the path to an investigation of human sexuality, in turning the searchlight of his implacable curiosity on an area that previous ages had kept in darkness, in his willingness to discuss the undiscussable, his effect was, in the end, a liberating one. He paved the way for those who would subsequently refute him—those who would see farther and more clearly. He served the evolution of romantic love in spite of himself.

The American Ideal: Individualism and Romantic Love

We have already observed the intimate connection between individualism and the ideal of romantic love (however conceived). This can help us to understand why that ideal first took hold—on a widespread social scale—in the United States, and why, even today, the ideal is regarded in many parts of the world as typically "American."

While attitudes toward sexuality were certainly dominated by the Puritan (later, Victorian) influence in American culture, and while the antiromantic "common sense" tradition in America often meant a denial of the importance of passion, still Americans, much more than others in the nineteenth century, were culturally free to marry for love—and thereby set an example for the rest of the Western world. As Burgess and Locke (1953) write in their historical survey *The Family: From Institution to Companionship,* "It is in the United States that perhaps the only, at any rate the most complete, demonstration of romantic love as the prologue and theme of marriage has been staged."

At the risk of being repetitive, it is necessary to stress once more that what was distinctive about the American outlook, and what represented a radical break with its European past, is, as we have seen, its unprecedented commitment to political freedom, its intransigent individualism, its doctrine of the supremacy of individual rights—and, more specifically, its belief in a person's right to pursue his or her own happiness *here on earth*. It is difficult for Americans today to appreciate fully the revolutionary significance of this concept, especially as seen from the perspective of European intellectuals. America has been correctly characterized as the first truly *secular* society in human history, for it was the first nation in the history of the world to view a human being not as a servant of a religious authority or of society or of the state, but as an entity with the right to exist for his or her own happiness. It was the first nation to give that principle explicit political expression.

In addition to philosophical and political considerations, the elevation of romantic love in American culture is explainable, perhaps, by the fact that America began, essentially, as an immigrant society whose members could more easily leave tradition behind; by the fact that the early frontier economy was inherently more adventuresome and wide open in its attitudes; and by the fact that the very roughness of early conditions put women at a premium, not merely sexually or economically, but on every possible level.

In the late nineteenth and early twentieth centuries, people were becoming more and more mobile, which led to an increasingly freer mingling of men and women in a wide variety of settings and contexts. The widespread availability of contraception and the increasing acceptance of divorce carried still further the liberation of man/woman relationships. The twentieth century has seen the declining influence of Victorian sexual attitudes, and, more recently, the growing understanding of female sexuality and the spreading recognition of the equality of men and women.

We who live in twentieth-century America enjoy unprecedented freedom in the conduct of our private lives, and in particular of our sexual lives. We are learning to see sex not as "the darker side" of our nature but as a normal expression of our total personality. We are less inclined to glamorize tragedy in the style of so many nineteenth-century Romanticists. As the influence of religion continues to decline, we feel less need to rebel and "prove" our "enlightenment" by means of debauchery. And as a consequence, the "naturalness" of romantic love is far more accepted today than ever before.

The Critics of Romantic Love

This does not mean that, in twentieth-century America, the ideal of romantic love has lacked critics. Quite the contrary. Many social and psychological observers have argued that the attempt to build a long-term relationship—marriage—on emotional foundations is, at best, grossly naive, and, at worst, pathological or socially irresponsible. Ralph Linton, an anthropologist, wrote in 1936:

> All societies recognize that there are occasional violent, emotional attachments between persons of opposite sex, but our present American culture is practically the only one which has attempted to ... make them the basis for marriage.... Their rarity in most societies suggests that they are psychological abnormalities to which our own culture has attached an extraordinary value.

A more elaborate and influential attack came in Denis de Rougemont's *Love in the Western World*, first published in 1940:

> No other civilization, in the 7,000 years that one civilization has been succeeding another, has bestowed on the love known as romance anything like the same amount of daily publicity.... No other civilization has embarked with anything like the same ingenuous assurance upon the perilous enterprise of making marriage coincide with love thus understood, and of making the first depend upon the second....
> In reality ... let romantic love overcome no matter how many obstacles, and it always fails at once. This is the obstacle constituted by time. Now, either marriage is an institution set up to be lasting—or it is meaningless.... To try to base marriage on a form of love which is unstable by definition is really to benefit the State of Nevada....

> Romance feeds on obstacles, short excitations, and partings; marriage, on the contrary, is made up of want, daily propinquity, growing accustomed to one another. Romance calls for "the far-away love" of the troubadour; marriage, for love of "one's neighbor."

In a still more fundamental attack, James H. S. Bossard and Eleanor S. Boll wrote in *Why Marriages Go Wrong* (1958):

> If one selects a mate and marries solely for personal happiness and personality fulfillment, then, when the mate no longer serves that function, the marriage is gone....
> The line between the individualist and the self-centered person is a very narrow one.... The desire for personal happiness degenerates into social lassitude....

To Bossard and Boll, American insistence on romantic love relationships reflects "a spoiled-child psychology."

Again, in a 1973 *Symposium on Love,* one participant expressed the views of many others when he suggested that

> On the socio-cultural level, as on the psychological, love may be like a crutch, impeding the development of new social forms so important for the development of a better and more satisfying human condition and society of the future.

Shifting to a more personal level of attack, it is interesting to consider a book published in 1965, called *The Significant Americans,* written by John F. Cuber and Peggy B. Harroff. Their book is described as "a study of sexual behavior among the affluent." In this study, the authors contrast two types of marriage, which they encountered: "Utilitarian marriage," characterized by an absence of mutual involvement or passion, held together by social, financial, and family considerations, made tolerable by long separations, immersion in "community activities," and sexual infidelity—and "Intrinsic marriage," characterized by passionate emotional and sexual involvement, a policy of sharing life experiences to the fullest extent possible, and an attitude of regarding the relationship as more interesting, more exciting, more fulfilling than any other aspect of social existence (in other words, romantic love). Partners in an "Intrinsic marriage" tend, according to the authors, to be very selfish with their time, in that they are reluctant to engage in social, political, community or other activities that would cause them to be separated, unless they are convinced there are very good reasons for doing so; they are clearly not looking for excuses to escape from each other. While this type of relationship tends to provoke some degree of envy from those who exist in a "Utilitarian marriage," according to the authors, it also provokes a good deal of resentment and hostility. The authors quote such hostile sentiments as "these immature people" must somehow "be brought into line." They quote a man trained in psychology as declaring, "Sooner or later you've just got to act your age. People who stay to themselves so much must have some psychological problems—if they don't, they'll soon develop them." They quote another psychologist as vigorously asserting, "Any man or woman who has to live *that* close is simply *sick*. He must need a mate as a crutch! He's too dependent! There's just something unhealthy about it." (These negative sentiments do *not* express views held by the authors of the book.)

Critics like to point out that the country in which romantic love found its best home is also the country with the highest divorce rate in the world. While a huge divorce rate is not inherently an indictment of romantic love (rather it suggests that many Americans are so committed to the ideal of happiness in marriage that they are unwilling to resign themselves to a life of suffering), it is unarguable that many, many people experience their efforts at romantic fulfillment as disappointing, if not disastrous failures. Disenchantment and disillusionment are undeniably widespread.

Open experiments with "swinging," "group marriage," sexual communes, multiple-couple families, three-person "marriages," all represent alternate pathways to personal fulfillment that more and more people seem to be exploring. But no one is claiming any exciting record of success. Variations in the structure of relationships do not seem to touch the essential issue. The problem clearly exists on a deeper level than such "solutions" address themselves to.

The overwhelming and undeniable reality of that problem—the difficulty of human beings achieving sustained happiness in an interpersonal relationship—dramatizes our need to think more deeply about love, and about what love and relationships depend on.

But first, let us pause to consider briefly why romantic love has been so severely criticized.

What Romantic Love is Not

Many of the commonest criticisms of romantic love are based on observing irrational or immature processes occurring between persons who profess to be "in love," and then generalizing to a repudiation of romantic love as such. In such cases, the arguments are not in fact directed against romantic love at all—not if one understands by romantic love "a passionate spiritual-emotional-sexual attachment between a man and a woman that reflects a high regard for the value of each other's person."

There are, for example, men and women who experience a strong sexual attraction for each other, conclude that they are "in love," and proceed to marry on the basis of their sexual attraction, ignoring the fact that they have few values or interests in common, have little or no genuine admiration for each other, are bound to each other predominantly by dependency needs, have incompatible personalities and temperaments, and, in fact, have little or no authentic interest in each other as persons. Of course such relationships are doomed to failure. They are not representative of romantic love, and it amounts to setting up a straw man to treat them as if they were.

To love a human being is to know and love his or her *person*. This presupposes the ability to see, and with reasonable clarity. It is commonly argued that romantic lovers manifest a strong tendency to idealize or glamorize their partners, to misperceive them, exaggerating their virtues and blinding themselves to their failings. Of course this sometimes occurs. But it is not inherent in the nature of love that it *must* occur. To argue that love is blind is to maintain that no real and deep affinities of a kind that inspire love can really exist between persons. This argument runs counter to the experience of men and women who do see the partner's weaknesses as well as strengths and who do love passionately.

Again, it is sometimes argued, as it is by de Rougemont (and, as we have seen, before him by Freud), that the experience of romantic love is generated solely by sexual frustrations and, therefore, must perish shortly after consummation. Frustration can create obsessive want and foster a tendency to endow a desired object with temporary value; yet anyone who argues that romantic love cannot survive sexual fulfillment is making an illuminating personal statement and is also revealing extraordinary blindness or indifference to the experience of others.

It is sometimes argued that since most couples do in fact suffer feelings of disenchantment shortly after marriage, the experience of romantic love must be a delusion. Yet many people experience disenchantment somewhere along the line in their careers, and it is not commonly suggested, therefore, that the pursuit of a meaningful career is a mistake. Many people experience some degree of disenchantment in their children, but it is not commonly supposed that the desire to have children is inherently immature and neurotic. Instead, it is generally recognized that the requirements for achieving happiness in one's career or success in child-rearing may be higher and more difficult than is ordinarily appreciated.

Romantic love is not omnipotent—and those who believe it is are too immature to be ready for it. Given the multitude of psychological problems that many people bring to a romantic relationship—given their doubts, their fears, their insecurities, their weak and uncertain self-esteem—given the fact that most have never learned that a love relationship, like every other value in life, requires consciousness, courage, knowledge, and wisdom to be sustained—it is not astonishing that most romantic relationships end disappointingly. But to indict romantic love on these grounds is to imply that, if "love is not enough"—if love of and by itself cannot indefinitely sustain happiness and fulfillment—then it is somehow in the wrong, is a delusion, even a neurosis. Surely the error lies, not in the *ideal* of romantic love, but in the irrational and impossible demands made of it.

It is very difficult to escape the feeling that at least some of the attacks on romantic love have their roots in nothing more complicated than envy, as the quotes given previously from *The Significant Americans* suggest: envy, personal unhappiness, and an inability to understand the psychology of persons whose capacity for the enjoyment of life is greater than one's own.

But there are deeper philosophical issues that need to be considered. Just as the advocacy of romantic love arose in a historicophilosophical context, so do many of the contemporary attacks.

We deal here, once again, with the tribal mentality—which means we are dealing once again with ethical and political theory. When reading many of the attacks on romantic love launched by contemporary intellectuals, I found myself haunted by the memory of the slogan stamped on Nazi coins: "The common good above the individual good." And by Hitler's declaration: "In the hunt for their own happiness, people fall all the more out of heaven into hell."

One of the tragedies of human history is that virtually all of the ethical systems that achieved any degree of world influence, were, at root, variations on the theme of self-sacrifice. Unselfishness was equated with virtue; selfishness—honoring the needs and wants of the self —was made a synonym of evil. With such systems, the individual has always been a victim, twisted against him or her self and commanded to be "unselfish" in sacrificial service to some allegedly higher value called God or pharaoh or emperor or king or society or the state or the race of the proletariat—or the cosmos.

It is a strange paradox of our history that this doctrine—which tells us that we are to regard ourselves, in effect, as sacrificial animals—has been generally accepted as a doctrine representing benevolence and love for mankind. One need only consider the consequences to which this has led to estimate the nature of its "benevolence." From the first individual, thousands of years ago, who was sacrificed on an altar for the good of the tribe, to the heretics and dissenters burned at the stake for the good of the populace or the glory of God, to the millions exterminated in gas chambers or slave-labor camps for the good of the race or of the proletariat, it is this morality that has served as justification for every dictatorship and every atrocity, past or present.

Yet few intellectuals have challenged the basic assumption which makes such slaughter possible—"the good of the individual must be subordinated to the good of the larger whole"—they fight over the particular applications of this principle; they fight over who should be sacrificed to whom and for whose benefit. They express horror and indignation when they do not approve of someone's particular choice of victims and beneficiaries; but they do not question the basic principle: that the individual is an object of sacrifice.

And so, in reviewing those attacks on romantic love which have to do with its neglect of the "higher good of the community," I found myself wondering how many more millions of human beings will have to suffer before we come to understand that there *is* no higher good than the good of the individual.

We shall return to the subject of love and selfishness later. But whatever solutions human beings must arrive at in order to obtain fulfillment in the context of man/woman relationships, the surrender of the right to the pursuit of personal happiness is not one of them.

To return, finally, to the curious criticism of romantic love with which this part of our discussion began— Linton's assertion that the rarity of romantic love in other cultures indicates that it may be a "psychological abnormality" of our own—we need only note that according to this logic we should have to condemn many other "abnormalities" of American civilization, such as its higher standard of living, its unparalleled recognition of individual rights, its greater degree of political freedom—all of which are indeed "rarities" elsewhere.

Relative to the rest of the world, the United States has been innovative in many areas. The importance it attaches to romantic love does indeed set it apart from many other cultures, but the educated classes in many of those cultures are looking to the American ideal with increasing longing.

On the Human-Potential Movement

Before returning to our central theme, I wish to take something of an excursion (a digression, perhaps) into territory that may appear remote from the subject of romantic love and yet which, in an indirect way, has a bearing on it. This has to do with the rise in this century of the human-potential movement.

Since here, too, we shall be dealing once again with the subject of individualism, let us begin by sharpening our understanding of its meaning. Individualism is at once an ethicopolitical concept and an ethicopsychological one. As an ethicopolitical concept, individualism upholds the supremacy of individual rights, the principle that a human being is an end in him- or herself, not a means to the ends of others, and that the proper goal of life is self-realization or self-fulfillment. As an ethicopsychological concept, individualism holds that a human being should think and judge independently, respecting nothing more than the sovereignty of his or her mind. It is intimately connected with the concept of autonomy (which I shall discuss later).

In addition to the social and cultural events described, the historical tide of individualism has given rise, during the past several decades, to a very significant phenomenon in the world of psychology—the "human-potential movement." This is at once a revolt against the narrow, reductionist view of the human person upheld by psychoanalysis and behaviorism, a reaching for a wider and more comprehensive understanding of the meaning of "human," and a reaching toward the "higher" possibilities of human nature.

In contrast to traditional psychology and psychiatry, which has been primarily concerned with "sickness" and the treatment of "illness," the human-potential movement is oriented toward all that lies on the other side of "normal," which pertains to growth, self-actualization (to actualize is to make real, to bring into reality), the exploration and fulfillment of positive potentialities.

Now what is especially interesting about this phenomenon, in the context of our discussion, is that the movement is under attack today for reasons remarkably similar to those given for some of the attacks on romantic love. It is alleged to be "self-centered," "self-indulgent," "a middle-class phenomenon"; and its exponents are accused of being indifferent, in their concern with self, to the problems "of the world as a whole."

The human-potential movement is definitely "a middle-class phenomenon"—just as was the first wide-scale acceptance of romantic love. Obviously persons who are struggling with the problem of physical survival, for whom disease and starvation are a daily issue, seldom concern themselves with "self-actualization." Such a concern is ordinarily experienced by those who have achieved a reasonable degree of material well-being and who want "more"—not more materially, but more spiritually, psychologically, emotionally, intellectually. The movement arose in an affluent society; it is an "American phenomenon."

Admittedly, there is a lot about this movement that is plain silly. The movement is rather comparable to a wild West frontier—a lot of enthusiasm, a few scattered sparks of genius, and a lot of people selling snake oil. It could hardly be otherwise. That is the common pattern of beginnings.

What is unfortunate is that many exponents of the human-potential movement have adopted increasingly apologetic and defensive postures in response to accusations of "selfishness." Of *course* the pursuit of self-actualization is selfish. So is the pursuit of physical health. So is the pursuit of sanity. So is the pursuit of happiness. So is the pursuit of your next breath of air.

Several thousand years of indoctrination in the ethics of self-sacrifice have made people terrified to acknowledge the obvious—that in their concern with personal growth they are motivated by self-interest *and are entitled to be;* and so we witness the unattractive spectacle of many exponents explaining that what they are *really* doing is preparing themselves, through "self-improvement," to be better servants of humanity, thereby conceding that only "social" justifications are acceptable.

One of the assumptions implicit in these attacks on the human-potential movement, which directly parallels some of the attacks on romantic love, is that a concern with self-actualization or personal fulfillment is inherently antisocial or socially irresponsible.

There is absolutely no foundation to such a claim and overwhelming evidence to support the contrary view. People who do not experience self-love have little or no capacity to experience love of others. People who are devoid of self-respect have little or no capacity to respect others. People who experience deep insecurities and self-doubts tend to experience other human beings as frightening and inimical. People who have little or no self have nothing to contribute to the world.

Indeed, if one looks at the history of human progress, at all the steps which have brought us from the cave to our present level of civilization, and of the genius, daring, courage, and creativity that made this progress possible—one cannot help but be struck by the fact of how much we owe to those whose lives were primarily given over to the task of discovering and fulfilling their own "destiny"—the artists, the scientists, the philosophers, the inventors, the industrialists whose life path was clearly one of self-actualization (self-development, self-fulfillment).

Looked at on its plus side, the human-potential movement has helped to create a fresh intellectual climate in which to approach the subject of romantic love. In opposing the reductionist-mechanist view of human nature (the view of human beings as machines), its proponents have brought back into psychology a new respect for such concepts as "mind," "consciousness," "choice," and "purpose." Discoveries in physics and biology have exploded old-fashioned materialism and have led inexorably toward what is frequently described as an *organismic* rather than a *mechanical* model of the universe. "Wholeness, organization, dynamics—these general conceptions may be stated as characteristics of the modern, as opposed to the mechanical, world-view of physics," writes Ludwig von Bertalanffy in *Problems of Life.*

Biology has never been able to do without such concepts as function, purpose, and consciousness; yet in recent decades they have gained increasingly in "respectability." The attempt to reduce a human being to a passive automaton, to interpret behavior, values, and choices as the mechanical products of societal and instinctual forces was *never* defensible; it ignored too much evidence, did violence to too much of human experience, and permitted itself too many non sequiturs—as philosophers were already pointing out even ahead of the new developments in physics and biology. The delusion that "the hard sciences" lend any support or credibility to reductionism is now vanishing.

In the context of the new understanding that is emerging, it is recognized that we can speak of "spiritual aspirations" and "spiritual affinities" without any theological, irrational, or prescientific implications. We are freer now to look at human beings and see what has always stared us in the face: that we are not machines—or that we are not "only" or "merely" machines.

Robots do not engage in romantic love. Neither do instinct-manipulated puppets. Neither, I will presume, do the favorite subject of behaviorists' investigation: rats and pigeons.

We are the most highly evolved species to develop on this planet. We have a consciousness unprecedented in its range and complexity. Our distinctive form of consciousness is the source of our specifically *human* needs and abilities. One of its manifestations is the experience of romantic love.

Romantic love is not a myth, waiting to be discarded, but, for most of us, a discovery, waiting to be born.

Needed: A New Understanding of Romantic Love

It is clear that "love is not enough."

The fact that two human beings love each other does not guarantee they will be able to create a joyful and rewarding relationship. Their love does not ensure their maturity and wisdom; yet without these qualities their love is in jeopardy. Their love does not automatically teach them communication skills or effective methods of conflict resolution, or the art of integrating their love into the rest of their existence; yet the absence of such knowledge can lead to the death of love. Their love does not produce self-esteem; it may reinforce it but it cannot create it; still without self-esteem love cannot survive.

And even among mature, well-actualized individuals, love is not necessarily "forever."

As people continue to grow and evolve, their needs and desires change or shift as to emphasis. New goals and longings can emerge, causing rifts in relationships. This does not mean—or need not mean—that love has "failed." A union that provides great joy, nourishment, and stimulation for two human beings is not a "failure" merely because it does not last forever; it can still be a great experience that one is glad to have lived.

When the marriage ritual that included the formula "till death do us part" was developed, few people could hope to survive their twenties. By the time a man died at the age of twenty-six he may easily have had three wives, two of whom died in childbirth. "Forever" had a different meaning in such a context than it has today for us, who can look forward to living into our seventies or eighties.

What creates the sense of failure, sometimes, is not that love does not produce joy and fulfillment for two human beings, but that they might not have known when it was time to let go; they fought to hold onto that which had already vanished, and the torment and frustration of their efforts they mistakenly call "the failure of romantic love."

So we need to rethink our understanding of romantic love—what it means, what kind of experience it affords, what needs it fulfills, and what conditions it depends on.

We need to see it of and by itself, as a unique encounter between man and woman, a unique experience and a unique adventure—possibly but not necessarily involving marriage, possibly but not necessarily involving children, possibly but not necessarily involving sexual exclusivity, possibly but not necessarily involving "till death do us part."

As we stand at this moment in history, we *are* in a

state of crisis with regard to romantic love, not because the ideal is irrational but because we are still in the process of grasping its meaning, still in the process of understanding its philosophical presuppositions and its psychological requirements.

Let us now explore in more detail the psychological roots of romantic love, the needs it strives to satisfy, and the conditions for success or failure. Let us consider what love is, why love is born, why it sometimes grows, and why it sometimes dies.

TWO

•

The Roots of Romantic Love

Prologue: First, a Self—Then a Possibility

When a man and a woman encounter each other in romantic love, seeking union, seeking fusion, seeking the experience of the most intimate contact, they come to each other from a context of aloneness. An understanding of this point is absolutely essential for everything that is to follow. Paradoxically, if we wish to understand romantic love, we must begin by understanding aloneness, the universal condition of us all.

In the beginning we are alone and do not yet know that we are alone. A newborn infant does not differentiate between self and nonself; there is no awareness of self, not, at any rate, as we who are adults experience such awareness.

To quote Mahler, Pine, and Bergman, in *The Psychological Birth of the Human Infant:*

> The biological birth of the human infant and the psychological birth of the individual are not coincident in time. The former is a dramatic, observable, and well-circumscribed event; the latter a slowly unfolding intrapsychic process.

Discovering boundaries—discovering where self ends and the external world begins—grasping and as-

57

similating the fact of *separateness*—is one of the foremost tasks of infancy, upon which normal development depends.

The second and overlapping part of this maturational process is *individuation:* the acquiring of those basic motor and cognitive skills, combined with a beginning sense of physical and personal identity, that represents the foundation of the child's autonomy (the child's capacity for inner direction, self-regulation, and self-responsibility). Separation and individuation mark the child's birth as a human being.

But these concepts apply not only to the early years of development. They have a wider meaning that continually manifests itself through the entire span of the human life cycle.

If we understand separation and individuation not as growth processes unique to infants but applicable to us all, we are able to see them as themes that recur on more and more advanced levels as the human organism matures and evolves. It is easy enough to see the basic pattern in a child's successful growth to adulthood—from learning to walk to selecting a career and establishing a home and a life. But we can see the same process at work in the struggles of a woman who is overidentified with the role of mother and who, when her child is grown, confronts the challenging question of who she is now that her child no longer is dependent on her; she, too, is engaged in a process of separation and individuation; she, too, is engaged in a struggle for autonomy. When a marriage ends in divorce or when a life partner of many years dies and a person must encounter the question of identity outside the context of the former relationship, once again what is involved is a process of separation and individuation.

We can strive to avoid the fact of our ultimate aloneness; it continually confronts us. A romantic-love relationship can nourish us; it cannot become a substitute for personal identity. When we attempt to deny these truths, it is our relationships that we corrupt—by dependency, by exploitation, by domination, by subservience, by our own unacknowledged terror.

Perhaps the essence of our evolution as human beings is to keep answering, on deeper and deeper levels, the basic question: "Who am I?" We answer that question, we define ourselves, through the acts of thinking, of feeling, and of doing—of learning to take more and more responsibility for our existence and well-being—and of expressing through our work and through our relationships more and more of who we are. This is the wider meaning of the concept of *individuation;* it represents a lifelong task.

When the child finds that his or her perceptions, feelings, or judgments conflict with those of parents or other family members, and the question arises of whether to heed the voice of self or to disown it in favor of the voice of others; when a woman believes that her husband is wrong on some fundamental issue, and the question arises of whether to express her thoughts or to suppress them and thus protect the "closeness" of the relationship; when an artist or scientist suddenly sees a path that would carry him or her far from the "consensual" beliefs and values of colleagues, far from the "mainstream" of contemporary orientation and opinion, and the question arises of whether to follow that lonely path wherever it leads, or to draw back, forget what was seen, and restrict his or her vision only to that which others can readily share—the issue in all such cases remains the same. Should one honor one's inner signals or disown them: autonomy versus conformity; self-expression versus self-repudiation; self-creation versus self-annihilation.

Innovators and creators are persons who can to a higher degree than average accept the condition of aloneness. They are more willing to follow their own vision, even when it takes them far from the mainland of the human community. Unexplored spaces do not frighten them—or not, at any rate, as much as they frighten those around them. This is one of the secrets of their power. That which we call "genius" has a great deal to do with courage and daring, a great deal to do with *nerve*.

Breathing is not a "social act." Neither is thinking. Of course we interact: We learn from others; we speak a common language, we express our thoughts, describe our fantasies, communicate about our feelings; we influence and affect one another. But consciousness by its nature is immutably private. *We are each of us, in the last analysis, islands of consciousness—and that is the root of our aloneness.*

To be alive is to be an individual. To be an individual who is conscious is to experience a unique perspective on the world, at least in some respects. To be an individual who is not only conscious but self-conscious is to encounter, if only for brief moments, if only in the privacy of one's own mind, the unalterable fact of one's aloneness.

Aloneness entails self-responsibility. No one can think for us, no one can feel for us, no one can live our life for us, and no one can give meaning to our existence except ourselves. To most people, this fact is terrifying. It may be the most fiercely resisted, the most passionately denied, fact of their being.

The forms their denial takes are endless: refusing to think and following uncritically the beliefs of others; disowning one's deepest feelings in order to "belong"; pretending to be helpless, pretending to be confused, pretending to be stupid, in order to avoid taking an independent stand; clinging to the belief that one will "die" if one does not have the love of this person or that; joining mass movements or "causes" that promise to spare one the responsibility of independent judgment and to obviate the need for a sense of personal identity; surrendering one's mind to a leader; killing and dying for symbols and abstractions that promise to grant glory and meaning to one's existence, with no effort required on one's own part save obedience; devoting all of one's energies to manipulating people into giving "love."

There are a thousand respects in which we are not alone, none of which stands in contradiction to the foregoing. As human beings, we are linked to all other members of the human community. As living beings, we are linked to all other forms of life. As inhabitants of the universe, we are linked to everything that exists. We stand within an endless network of relationships. Separation and connectedness are polarities, with each entailing the other.

We are all parts of one universe, true enough. But within that universe we are each of us a single point of consciousness, a unique event, a private, unrepeatable world.

If we do not understand this, we cannot understand some of our most enrapturing experiences of union and fusion. We cannot understand those extraordinary moments of serenity and bliss when we feel ourselves to be one with all that exists. And we cannot understand the ecstasy of romantic love.

The tragic irony of people's lives (this point can hardly be stressed enough) is that the very attempt to deny aloneness results in denying love. Without an "I" who loves, what is the meaning of love?

First, a self—then, a possibility: the exquisite joy of one self encountering another.

Toward a Definition of Love

We are not yet ready to approach romantic love directly. We must begin with an examination of love in general—love as such. Romantic love is a special case within this wider category. We can feel many different kinds of love, from romantic love to the love that exists between parents and children to the love of friends to the love of a human for an animal, and so forth. But there are certain observations that apply to *all* kinds of love, certain truths universal to love as such, and they are the necessary foundation of any subsequent discussion of romantic love.

Love is, in the most general sense, our emotional

response to that which we value highly. As such, it is the experience of joy in the existence of the loved object, joy in proximity, and joy in interaction or involvement. To love is to delight in the being whom one loves, to experience pleasure in that being's presence, to find gratification or fulfillment in contact with that being. We experience the loved being as a source of fulfillment for profoundly important needs. (Someone we love enters the room; our eyes and heart light up. We look at this person; we experience a rising sense of joy within us. We reach out and touch; we feel happy, fulfilled.)

But love is more than an emotion; it is a judgment or evaluation, and an action tendency. Indeed, *all* emotions entail evaluations and action tendencies.

The first thing we must recognize about emotions is that they are value responses. *They are automatic psychological responses, involving both mental and physiological features, to our subconscious appraisal of what we perceive as the beneficial or harmful relationship of some aspect of reality to ourselves.*

If we pause to consider any emotional response, from love to fear to rage, we can notice that implicit in every response is a *dual* value judgment. Every emotion reflects the judgment of "for me" or "against me"—and also "to what extent." Thus, emotions differ according to their *content* and according to their *intensity*. Strictly speaking, these are not two *separate* value judgments; they are integral aspects of the same judgment and are experienced as one response.

Love is the highest, the most intense, expression of the assessment "for me," "good for me," "beneficial to my life." (In the person of someone we love we see, in extraordinarily high measure, many of those traits and characteristics that we feel are most appropriate to life—life as we understand and experience it—and therefore most desirable for our own well-being and happiness.)

Every emotion contains an inherent action tendency; that is, an impetus to perform some action related to that particular emotion. The emotion of fear is a person's response to that which threatens his or her values; it entails the action tendency to avoid or flee from the feared object. The emotion of love entails the action tendency to achieve some form of contact with the loved being, some form of interaction or involvement. (Sometimes a lover will complain, understandably, that, "You say you love me, but I could never tell it *from your actions*. You don't want to spend time alone with me, you don't want to talk with me, so how would you *act differently* if you *didn't* love me?")

Finally, and in a sense more fundamentally, we may describe love as representing an *orientation,* an attitude or psychological state with regard to the loved being, deeper and more enduring than any moment-by-moment alteration of feeling or emotion. As an orientation, *love represents a disposition to experience the loved being as the embodiment of profoundly important personal values—and, as a consequence, a real or potential source of joy.*

Love Between Parent and Child: A Special Case

Aristotle suggests that if we wish to understand love we should take as our "model" relationship—by which to measure, compare and contrast other relationships—the attachment that exists between *friends* who are more or less equal in development and who are joined by common values, common interests, and by mutual admiration. We shall see, as we move more deeply into the nature of love, that this viewpoint has a great deal to recommend it, and nowhere more so than when thinking about romantic love.

But curiously enough, a very different relationship, the relationship of child and parent, is sometimes regarded as the ideal point of reference from which to grasp the essence of love—and, for that matter, "healthy" or "desirable" human relationships in general. This, for example, is the position taken by anthropologist Ashley Montagu, who writes, "It has, I believe, universally been acknowledged that the mother-infant relationship perhaps more than any other defines the very essence of love." I regard this perspective as about as mistaken as it is possible to be and I want to say a few words about my reasons.

To begin with, if one studies the analysis of love offered by philosophers and psychologists across the centuries, and the many controversies surrounding their positions, it is obvious that Montagu's viewpoint has been anything but "universally acknowledged." It is, however, held by enough people to be worth refuting.

Montagu leads us to his conclusion by way of the following observation:

> From the moment of birth the baby needs the reciprocal exchange of love with its mother. From the very onset the baby is capable of conferring great benefits upon the mother—*if* the maternal-infant relationship is not disturbed.... [If] the baby is left with the mother and put to nurse at her breast, three problems which ... have been responsible for much tragedy and unhappiness are in most cases solved at once.... Hemorrhaging from the womb after birth ... is reduced and the uterus begins its return to almost normal size within a matter of minutes, and the placenta becomes detached and is ejected.... The baby is in turn, of course, also benefitted....
> ... Bearing in mind ... benefits which accrue to mother and child, perhaps we could ... say that *love is the relationship between persons which contributes to the welfare and development of each.*

That mutual benefits, physiological and psychological, are exchanged between infant and mother is undeniable. It is equally true that if I buy a book and pay for it, and the bookstore owner uses part of his earnings to support his own continuing education, ours has clearly been a relationship in which each contributed to the welfare and development of the other. It does not follow that the bookstore owner and I love each other. So it is immediately clear that Montagu's definition lacks something essential.

Moreover, while the mother *intends* to benefit the infant, the infant does not *intend* to benefit the mother. The infant is not even aware, initially, of the mother as a separate being. In what sense, then, can the infant be said to "love" the mother?

Observe that this particular relationship is the ultimate instance of a relationship between *unequals*. It is a relationship in which, on the level of conscious intention, one party is almost entirely the giver, and the other party is almost entirely the receiver. Such a relationship, when existing between adults, is generally regarded as exploitative and parasitical—although it is not, of course, so regarded between infant and mother, for obvious biological reasons.

The significance of the child-parent relationship, relative to our understanding of love in general and romantic love in particular, is of a very different order.

The mother or mother surrogate is the first representative of humanity in the child's life. Here the infant can gain a sense of security, of safety. Here the infant can learn to experience trust. Here it can learn to experience another human being as a source of pleasure and gratification. Such experiences are a highly valuable *preparation* for love. Ideally, what the child is acquiring is an emotional foundation for the ability to love. But this should not be confused with the experience of love itself, which requires a level of maturity beyond that of an infant.

And even later, when the child has developed to the point of being able to love in an active sense, the child-parent relationship remains too much of a "special case" to serve as a prototype for love in general. What remains, at least until adulthood, is the problem of inequality, with all the limitations inequality imposes.

The Need and the Desire to Love

In seeking to understand romantic love, we want to understand the particular psychological needs that romantic love fulfills. And we want to understand the roots of those needs.

Let us consider our need for human *companionship,* our need for people we can respect, admire, and value, and interact with in a variety of ways and on various levels of our being. Virtually everyone experiences the desire for companionship, friendship, and love as a given of human nature, requiring no explanation. Sometimes, a pseudoexplanation is offered, in terms of an alleged "gregarious instinct" that human beings are said to possess. But this illuminates nothing.

We could say that our desire for companionship is explained in part by the fact that living and dealing with other persons in a social context, trading goods and services, and the like, affords us a manner of survival immeasurably superior to that which we could obtain by ourselves on a desert island or on a self-sustaining farm. We obviously find it to our interest to deal with men and women whose values and character are, in important respects, like our own, rather than with men and women of inimical values and character. And, normally, we develop feelings of benevolence or affection toward people who share our values and who act in ways that are beneficial to our existence. It is easy enough to see, however, that such a response does not address itself to the fundamental question, and that practical, existential considerations such as these are not sufficient to account for the phenomenon about which we are inquiring.

The desire for companionship and love rises out of more *intimate* considerations, reflecting at their root motives that are more psychological than existential. Almost everyone is aware of the desire for companionship, for someone to talk to, to be with, to feel understood by, to share experiences with—the desire for *emotional closeness and intimacy with another human being*—although there are, of course, great differences in the intensity with which different people experience this desire.

Let us focus first on the need and desire *to love*. The origin of our desire to love lies in our profound need *to value,* to find things in the world which we can care about, can feel excited and inspired by. It is our values that tie us to the world and that motivate us to go on living. Every action is taken for the purpose of gaining or protecting something we believe will benefit our life or enhance our experience.

If a person were to grow from infancy utterly incapable of finding anything nourishing, beneficial, or pleasurable in the environment, what would inspire such a person to persevere in the struggle for existence? Would not growth and development be stopped at the very beginning? A person who cares about nothing does not care to live.

Life is worthwhile—at any age—precisely to the extent that we find particular values worth pursuing. A child who can find nothing in the environment that is a source of pleasure, nothing to which the child can respond to affirmatively, with interest, curiosity, and excitement, is almost certainly doomed. Such a child could not survive the first years of life.

Children need to find joy in their world, joy in various activities, joy in different aspects of their physical surroundings, and the promise of joy in association with other human beings. The child is an active force, not merely a passive recipient. The child's need to love can be as powerful as—if not more powerful than—the need to receive love. And this becomes no less true as we mature.

As adults, many of us have known the pain of a capacity for love that did not have an outlet. We wish to experience admiration; we long for the sight of human beings and achievements we can truly enjoy and respect. And if this longing is not satisfied, we feel alienation, depression. We live in the world; we wish to believe in the possibilities of the world. We are alive; we wish to see the triumph of life. We are human; we wish to associate with representatives of humanity who inspire.

If we have a healthy level of self-esteem, we are more likely to be consciously aware of this issue. If we suffer from deep insecurities, this need may become distorted by problems of envy, jealousy, or resentment toward those who are more fulfilled than ourselves. But the need continues to exist.

I am thinking of the sadness I have sometimes heard expressed by persons who attain success after years of a difficult struggle and who, contrary to their dreams and expectations, found the people they met "at the top" in no way more interesting or inspiring than those they had encountered earlier. I am thinking of the painful longing which highly talented and accomplished people sometimes express for the sight of someone or something to which they can respond with passionate admiration.

In this respect we are all children—hoping to find in the world around us those lights that will at once illuminate our journey and make the struggle worth the effort.

One of the values of passionate love is that it allows us to exercise our capacity to love; it provides a channel for our energy; it is a source of inspiration, a blessing on existence, a confirmation of the value of life.

But the desire to love, as well as the desire to be loved, contains still other elements. Let us look further.

At the Core of Romantic Love: The Muttnik Principle

At this point, I wish to give an account of two incidents in my own life that were crucial for my understanding of love and human relationships. I have told this story, more briefly, in *The Psychology of Self-*

Esteem. Here, a more amplified version, with additional commentary, is necessary. I do not know of any more effective way to bring us to what I believe is the core significance of romantic love.

We shall be dealing here with what I first called the Muttnik Principle and later, more formally, called the Principle of Psychological Visibility. An intense experience of *mutual psychological visibility* is, as we shall see, at the very center of romantic love. Let us see what this means and how and why it is so.

One afternoon in 1960, while sitting alone in the living room of my apartment, I found myself contemplating with pleasure a large philodendron plant standing against a wall. It was a pleasure I had experienced before, but suddenly it occurred to me to wonder: What is the nature of this pleasure? What is its cause?

During that period I would not describe myself as "a nature lover," although I subsequently became one. At the time I was aware of positive feelings that accompanied my contemplation of the philodendron; I was unable to explain them.

The pleasure was not primarily aesthetic. Were I to learn that the plant was artificial, its aesthetic characteristics would remain the same but my response would change radically; the special pleasure I experienced would vanish. It seemed clear that essential to my enjoyment was the knowledge that the plant was healthily and glowingly *alive.* There was a feeling of a bond, almost a kind of kinship, between the plant and me; surrounded by inanimate objects, we were united in the fact of possessing life. I thought of the motive of people who, in the most impoverished conditions plant flowers in boxes on their windowsills—for the pleasure of watching something grow. Apparently, observing successful life is of value to human beings.

Suppose, I thought, I were on a dead planet where I had every material provision to ensure survival but where nothing was alive. I would feel like a metaphysical alien. Then suppose I came upon a living plant.

Surely I would greet the sight with eagerness and pleasure. *Why?*

Because, I realized, all life—life by its very nature—entails a struggle, and struggle entails the possibility of defeat; we desire and find pleasure in seeing concrete instances of successful life as confirmation of our knowledge that successful life is possible. It is, in effect, a *metaphysical* experience. We desire the sight, not necessarily as a means of allaying doubts or of reassuring ourselves, but as a means of experiencing and confirming on the perceptual plane, the level of immediate reality, that which we know abstractly, conceptually.

If such is the value a plant can offer to a human being, I mused, then the sight of another being can offer a much more intense form of this experience. The successes and achievements of those around us, in their own persons and in their work, can provide fuel and inspiration for our efforts and strivings. Perhaps this is one of the greatest gifts human beings can offer one another. A greater gift than charity, a greater gift than any explicit teaching or any words of advice—the sight of happiness, achievement, success, fulfillment.

The next crucial step in my thinking occurred on an afternoon, some months later, when I sat on the floor playing with my dog, a wirehaired fox terrier named Muttnik.

We were jabbing at and boxing with each other in mock ferociousness. What I found delightful and fascinating was the extent to which Muttnik appeared to grasp the playfulness of my intention. She was snarling and snapping and striking back while being unfailingly gentle in a manner that projected total, fearless trust. The event was not unusual; it is one with which most dog owners are familiar. But a question suddenly occurred to me, of a kind I had never asked myself before: Why am I having such an enjoyable time? What is the nature and source of my pleasure?

Part of my response, I recognized, was simply the pleasure of watching the healthy self-assertiveness of a living entity. But that was not the essential factor causing my response. That factor pertained to the interaction between the dog and myself, a sense of interacting and communicating with a living consciousness.

If I were to view Muttnik as an automaton without consciousness or awareness and to view her actions and responses as entirely mechanical, then my enjoyment would vanish. The factor of consciousness was of primary importance.

Then I thought once again of being marooned on an uninhabited island. Muttnik's presence there would be of enormous value to me, not because she could make any practical contribution to my physical survival, but because she offered a form of *companionship*. She would be a conscious entity to interact and communicate with—as I was doing now. *But why is that of value?*

The answer to this question, I realized, with a rising sense of excitement, would explain much more than the attachment to a pet. Involved in this issue is the psychological principle that underlies our desire for *human* companionship—the principle that would explain why a conscious entity seeks out and values other conscious entities, *why consciousness is a value to consciousness*.

When I identified the answer I called it the "Muttnik Principle" because of the circumstances under which it was discovered. Let us consider the nature of this principle.

The key to understanding my pleasurable reaction to playing with Muttnik was in the self-awareness that came from the nature of the feedback she was providing. From the moment that I began to "box," she responded in a playful manner; she conveyed no sign of feeling threatened; she projected an attitude of trust and pleasure and pleasurable excitement. Were I to push or jab at an inanimate object, it would react in a purely mechanical way; it would not be responding to *me;* there could be no possibility of its grasping the meaning of my actions, of apprehending my intentions, and of guiding its behavior accordingly. Such communication and response are possible only among conscious entities. The effect of Muttnik's behavior was to make me feel *seen*, to make me feel *psychologically visible* (to a modest extent). Muttnik was responding to me, not as a mechanical object, but as a person.

And, as part of the same process, I was experiencing a greater degree of visibility *to myself;* I was making contact with a playfulness in my personality which, during those years, I generally kept severely contained, so the interaction also contained elements of *self-discovery,* a theme to which I shall return shortly.

What is significant and must be stressed is that Muttnik was responding to me as a person in a way that I regarded as objectively appropriate, that is, in accordance with my view of myself and of what I was conveying to her. Had she responded with fear and an attitude of cowering, I would have experienced myself as being, in effect, misperceived by her and would not have felt pleasure.

While the example of an interaction between a human being and a dog may appear very primitive, I believe that it reflects a pattern that is manifest, potentially, between any two consciousnesses able to respond to each other. All positive interactions between human beings produce the experience of visibility to a degree. The climax of that possibility is achieved in romantic love, as we shall see shortly.

So we must consider the question: Why do we value and find pleasure in the experience of self-awareness and psychological visibility that the appropriate response or feedback from another consciousness can evoke?

Consider the fact that we normally experience ourselves, in effect, as a process—in that consciousness itself is a process, an activity, and the contents of our mind are a shifting flow of perceptions, images, organic sensations, fantasies, thoughts, and emotions. Our mind is not an unmoving entity which we can contemplate objectively—that is, contemplate as a direct object of experience—as we contemplate objects in the external world.

We normally have, of course, a sense of ourselves, of our own identity, but it is experienced more as a feeling than a thought—a feeling which is very diffuse, which is interwoven with all our other feelings, and which is very hard, if not impossible, to isolate and consider by itself. Our "self-concept" is not a single concept, but a cluster of images and abstract perspectives on our various (real or imagined) traits and characteristics, the sum total of which can never be held in focal awareness at any one time; that sum is experienced, but it is not *perceived* as such.

In the course of our life, our values, goals, and ambitions are first conceived in our mind; that is, they exist as data of consciousness, and then—to the extent that our life is successful—are translated into action and objective reality. They became part of the "out there," of the world that we perceive. They achieve expression and reality in material form. This is the proper and necessary pattern of human existence. *To live successfully is to put ourselves into the world, to give expression to our thoughts, values, and goals.* Our life is unlived precisely to the extent that this process fails to occur.

Yet our most important value—our character, soul, psychological self, spiritual being—whatever name one wishes to give it—can never follow this pattern in a literal sense, can never exist apart from our own consciousness. It can never be perceived by us as part of the "out there." But we *desire* a form of objective self-awareness and, in fact, *need* this experience.

Since we are the motor of our own actions, since our concept of who we are, of the person we have evolved, is central to all our motivation, we desire and need the fullest possible experience of the reality and objectivity of that person, of our self.

When we stand before a mirror, we are able to perceive our own face as an object in reality, and we normally find pleasure in doing so, in contemplating the physical entity that is ourself. There is a value in being able to look and think, "That's me." The value lies in the experience of objectivity.

To say it once again: The externalization of the objectification of the internal is of the very nature of successful life. We wish to see our *self* included in this process.

And, in an *indirect* sense, it *is,* every time we act on our judgment, every time we say what we think or feel or mean, every time we honestly express through word and deed our internal reality, our inner being.

But in a *direct* sense? Is there a mirror in which we can perceive our *psychological* self? In which we can, as it were, perceive our own soul? Yes. The mirror is another consciousness.

As individuals alone, we are able to know ourselves conceptually—at least to some extent. What another consciousness can offer is the opportunity for us to experience ourselves perceptually, as concrete objects "out there."

Of course, some people's consciousnesses are so alien to our own that the "mirrors" they provide yield the wildly distorted reflections of an amusement park's chamber of horrors. The experience of significant visibility requires consciousnesses congruent, to some meaningful extent, with our own.

Here is the limitation of Muttnik, or of any lower animal. True enough, in her response I was able to see reflected a small aspect of my own personality. But we can experience optimal self-awareness and visibility only in a relationship with a conciousness possessing an equal range of awareness, that is, another human being.

A word of clarification seems necessary at this point. I do not wish to imply that first we acquire a sense of identity entirely independent of any human relationships, and *then* seek the experience of visibility in interaction with others. Our self-concept is not the creation of others, as some writers have suggested, but obviously our relationships and the responses and feedback we receive contribute to the sense of self we acquire. All of us, to a profoundly important extent, experience who we are in the context of our relationships. When we encounter a new human being our personality contains, among other things, the consequences of many past encounters, many experiences, the internalization of many responses and instances of feedback from others. And we keep growing and evolving *through our encounters*.

In successful romantic love, there is a unique depth of absorption by, and fascination with, the being and personality of the partner. Hence there can be, for each, a uniquely powerful experience of visibility. Even if this state is not realized optimally, it may still be realized to an unprecedented degree. And this is one of the main sources of the excitement—and nourishment—of romantic love.

But much more needs to be said about the *process* of psychological visibility—how it is engendered and what it entails.

Our basic premises and values, our sense of life, the level of our intelligence, our characteristic manner of processing experience, our basic biological rhythm, and other features commonly referred to as "temperament"—all are made manifest in our personality. "Personality" is the externally perceivable sum of all of the psychological traits and characteristics that distinguish a human being from all other human beings.

Our psychology is expressed through behavior, through the things we say and do, and through the ways we say and do them. It is in this sense that our self is an object of perception to others. When others react to us, to their view of us and of our behavior, their perception is in turn expressed through *their* behavior, by the way they look at us, by the way they speak to us, by the way they respond, and so forth. If their view of us is consonant with our deepest vision of who we are (which may be different from whom we profess to be), and if their view is transmitted by their behavior, we feel perceived, we feel psychologically visible. We experience a sense of the objectivity of our self and of our psychological state of being. We perceive the reflection of our self in their behavior. It is in this sense that others can be a psychological mirror.

More precisely, this is one of the senses in which others can be a psychological mirror. There is another.

When we encounter a person who thinks as we do, who notices what we notice, who values the things we value, who tends to respond to different situations as we do, not only do we experience a strong sense of affinity with such a person but also we can experience our self through our perception of that person. This is another form of the experience of objectivity. This is another manner of perceiving our self in the world, external to consciousness, as it were. And as such, this is another form of experiencing psychological visibility. The pleasure and excitement that we experience in the presence of such a person, with whom we can enjoy this sense of affinity, underscores the importance of the need that is being satisfied.

The experience of visibility, then, is not merely a function of how another individual responds to us. It is also a function of how that individual responds to the world. These considerations apply equally to all instances of visibility, from the most casual encounter to the most intense love affair.

Just as there are many different aspects to our personality and inner life, so we may feel visible in different respects in various human relationships. We may experience a greater or lesser degree of visibility, or a wider or narrower range, of our total personality, depending on the nature of the person with whom we are dealing and on the nature of our interaction.

Sometimes, the aspect in which we feel visible pertains to a basic character trait; sometimes, to the nature of our intention in performing some action; sometimes, to the reasons behind a particular emotional response; sometimes, to an issue involving our sense of life; sometimes, to a matter concerning our work; sometimes, to our sexual psychology; sometimes, to our aesthetic values. The range of possibilities is almost inexhaustible.

All the forms of interaction and communication among people—spiritual, intellectual, emotional, physical—combine to give us the perceptual evidence of our visibility in one respect or another; or, relative to particular people, can produce in us the impression of invisibility. Most of us are largely unaware of the process by which this occurs; we are aware only of the results. We are aware that, in the presence of a particular person, we do or do not feel "at home," do or do not feel a sense of affinity or understanding or emotional attachment.

The mere fact of holding a conversation with another human being entails a marginal experience of visibility, if only the experience of being perceived as a conscious entity. However, in intimate human relationships, with a person we deeply admire and care for, we expect a far more profound visibility, involving highly individual and personal aspects of our inner life.

I shall have more to say about the determinants of visibility in any particular relationship. But it is fairly obvious that a significant mutuality of intellect, of basic premises and values, of fundamental attitude toward life, is the precondition of that projection of mutual visibility which is the essence of authentic friendship, or, above all, of romantic love. A friend, said Aristotle, is another self. This is precisely what lovers experience to the most intense degree. In loving you, I encounter myself. A lover ideally reacts to us as, in effect, we would react to our self in the person of another. Thus, we perceive our self through our lover's reaction. We perceive our own person through its consequences in the consciousness—and, as a result, in the behavior of our partner.

Here, then, we can discern one of the main roots of the human desire for companionship, for friendship and for love: *the desire to perceive our self as an entity in reality, to experience the perspective of objectivity through and by means of the reactions and response of other human beings.*

The principle involved, the Muttnik Principle—let us call it the Principle of Psychological Visibility—may be summarized as follows: *Human beings desire and need the experience of self-awareness that results from perceiving the self as an objective existent, and they are able to achieve this experience through interaction with the consciousness of other living beings.*

Visibility and Self-Discovery

When we discuss psychological visibility we are always operating within the context of degree. From childhood on, we receive from human beings some measure of appropriate feedback; every child experiences some degree of visibility. Without it, a child could not survive. A statistically few and fortunate children experience a high degree of visibility from adults in their early years. Working with clients in the context of psychotherapy and with students at my Intensives on *Self-Esteem and the Art of Being,* I am struck over and over again by the frequency with which the agony of invisibility in their homelife as children is clearly central to their developmental problems and to their insecurities and inadequacies in their love relationships.

As a child grows, to the extent that growth is successful, the reactions and responses of others open the door to various self-observations that contribute in a positive way to the elaboration of the child's self-concept; sometimes these observations go beyond what the child knows or believes to be true. Visibility often entails self-discovery.

And this same theme plays a paramount role in adult relationships. An intimate relationship, in which we feel truly seen by another human being, always entails at various points elements of self-discovery, the awareness of hitherto unrecognized capacities, latent potentialities, character traits that never surfaced to the level of explicit recognition, and so forth.

I remember the first time I fell in love, when I was eighteen years old. I felt enormous pleasure and excitement in finding someone with whom I could share important values and interests. I experienced a greater sense of psychological visibility than I had ever known before. At the same time, and as part of the same process, my consciousness of who I was *expanded*. Because the "someone" in question was a female, our interaction led to deepening contact with my own maleness, with a corresponding enlargement of my sense of self.

A sustained experience of visibility in a relationship irresistibly generates contact with new dimensions of who we are. When visibility goes to any significant depth, and especially when it lasts across a significant period of time, it always stimulates the process of self-discovery. This is one of the most exciting elements in any human encounter—the possibility of this expanded awareness of self. If I think back on any of the significant relationships in my life that followed this first love affair, I see that each one of them took me to a deeper and deeper understanding of who I was.

In the fifteen years of my relationship with Patrecia, both before and after we were married, I felt myself to be engaged in a continuous voyage of self-exploration. It was a mutual process and it seemed to me to be of the very essence of our interactions. It was an adventure, the challenge of always seeing deeper and deeper into each other.

When we met, Patrecia lived 'in her body" to a far greater extent than I did and was in far better touch with her feelings; her emotional openness and willingness to be transparent facilitated the process of my own deepening contact with my inner life. Through her, I learned the power of vulnerability, the power of letting others see who I was and what I felt, without defense or apology. I rediscovered the child in myself—not only because she was in contact with the child in herself, but also because she saw very clearly the child in me. Paradoxically, at the same time, I came to a deeper understanding of my ruthlessness, and allowed Patrecia to discover hers. "I love the woman in you," she would sometimes say, and she helped me integrate a part of myself I had not known about. Sometimes I would become upset over some issue that I was, in fact, perfectly capable of handling, and she would say, "Stop trying to pretend you're not Nathaniel Branden." Once, early in our relationship, she said to me, "Sometimes you're really awfully arrogant." I asked, "How do you feel about that?" She answered, "Well, I think I like it, because it gives me the nerve to accept that part of myself." When she died, and I was saying good-bye for the last time, the only words I could utter were, "Thank you. Thank you. Thank you."

And now, as I sit at my desk, writing these words, I see her face grinning at me—she is almost laughing—and she seems to be saying, "Are you writing this because it really helps to clarify your point, or are you trying to smuggle in a love letter to me?" "I'm not totally certain, Patrecia." "Well, leave it in. Sometimes when you're eager to explain some point you can get a little abstract and remote. Let them have *you,* not just your ideas."

Visibility—or Pseudovisibility?

When two human beings encounter each other, the *willingness* and *ability* of each person genuinely to *see* the other determines, at the most fundamental level, the degree to which each will experience visibility.

Beyond that, however, we can name two factors that are clearly basic. One is the extent of the mutuality of mind and values that exists between the two persons, the extent to which they are similar in outlook, in orientation toward life, in the development of their consciousness. The other is the extent to which the self-concept of each corresponds with reasonable accuracy to the actual facts of his or her psychology, the extent to which each knows and perceives him or herself realistically, the extent to which the inner view of self conforms to the personality projected by behavior.

As an example of the first of these two factors, suppose that a self-confident and healthily assertive woman encounters an anxious, hostile, and insecure man. The man reacts to her with suspiciousness and antagonism; whatever she says or does is interpreted by him malevolently. He sees her self-assurance as the wish to control and dominate him. In such a case, the woman does not feel visible; she may feel bewildered or mystified or indignant at being so grossly misperceived. In truth, he can hardly be said to be seeing her at all; the gulf between their orientations is too great. Now suppose that another man, witnessing their encounter, smiles at her in a way that signals his understanding of her feelings and his support; she relaxes, she smiles back—suddenly she feels visible.

As an example of the second factor, suppose a man is inclined to rationalize his own behavior and to support his *pretense* at self-esteem by means of totally unrealistic fantasies. His self-deceiving image of the kind of person he is conflicts inevitably with the actual self conveyed to others by his actions. The consequence is that he feels chronically frustrated and chronically invisible in human relationships, because the feedback he receives is not compatible with his pretensions. Ironically, were someone to "buy his act," it would not make him feel visible either, since there is no way for him to avoid knowing, somewhere in his psyche, that his act is not him. (But if, without condemnation or contempt, someone would see past this act, would see to the root of the insecurity that generates his felt need for an act, such a person would have the power to afford him the experience of actual visibility.)

Sometimes, in a case of interactions between two immature people, both of whom have lives built on massive pretensions, a kind of *illusion* of visibility can be mutually projected, in a situation where each participant supports the pretensions and self-deceptions of the other, in exchange for receiving such support "in trade." The "trade," of course, occurs on a subconscious level, more or less. Interestingly enough, in such relationships—and they are hardly uncommon—there is an *actual* experience of visibility underlying what may be termed the surface pseudovisibility. Deep in the psyche of each participant is the awareness that one's partner knows exactly what is going on. They can relate and reinforce each other by a kind of silent, unspoken understanding. I would denominate such a relationship not as romantic love but as *immature love,* which we shall need to examine in more detail later.

These examples isolate the essence of a process. They do not convey, and are not intended to convey, the full complexity of an actual human relationship where often authentic visibility and pseudovisibility, real traits and fantasy traits, blend and intermingle along a continuum—with optimal realism at one end, and almost total self-deception at the other.

Visibility and Understanding

Our desire for love from others is inseparable from our desire for visibility. If someone professed to love us but when in talking about what he or she found lovable named characteristics we did not think we possessed, did not especially admire, and could not personally relate to, we would hardly feel nourished or loved. We do not wish to be loved blindly; we wish to be loved for specific reasons. And if another professes to love us for reasons that do not bear any relation to our self-perceptions or values or standards, we do not feel gratified, we do not even feel really loved, because we do not feel visible; we do not feel that the other person is responding to *us.*

The desire for visibility is often experienced as the desire to receive understanding. If I am happy and proud of some achievement, I want to feel that those who are close to me, those I care for, understand my achievement and its personal meaning to me, understand and attach importance to the reasons behind my emotions. Or, if I am given a book by a friend and told that this is the kind of book I will enjoy, I feel pleasure and gratification if my friend's judgment proves correct, because then I feel visible, I feel understood. Or, if I suffer over some personal loss, it is of value to me to know that my plight is understood by those close to me, and that my emotional state has reality for them.

I felt more loved by Patrecia than I had ever felt before. I also felt better understood. To feel understood is the essence of visibility. I find myself recalling an occasion at a party, many years ago, when someone was complimenting me in a very obsequious and self-abnegating way; after the man left, Patrecia said to me, "It must be very uncomfortable for you—so often receiving what they think are compliments from people who are so frightened and insecure. I wanted to tell him to go away. To him I'm sure you looked polite and compassionate. To me you looked young and lonely."

For any mature individual, "blind" love may help to quell anxiety, but it will not answer our hunger to feel visible. It is not unconditional and unseeing support that we need, but *consciousness,* perception, and understanding.

The experience of visibility may entail receiving sympathy, or empathy, or compassion, or respect, or appreciation, or admiration, or love, or almost any combination of the foregoing. Visibility does not necessarily entail love. But "love" devoid of visibility is delusion.

The Desire for Validation

Sometimes people confuse the desire to feel seen, or visible, with the desire to be "validated." They are not the same thing.

The desire to be validated, confirmed, approved of, in one's being and behavior, is normal. We are inclined to call such a desire pathological only when it gains such ascendancy in one's hierarchy of values that one will sacrifice honesty and integrity in order to achieve it, in which case one clearly suffers from lack of self-esteem. But even in its most normal and realistic manifestations, we need to distinguish between that desire and the desire for visibility—even though, on the level of direct experience, there is doubtless some "spillover" effect.

The desire for visibility is by no means an expression of a weak or uncertain ego, or of low self-esteem. On the contrary, the lower our self-esteem, the more we feel the need to hide, the more ambivalent our feelings toward visibility are likely to be: we both long for and are terrified by it. The more we take pride in who we are, the more transparent we are willing to be. I might almost add: the more transparent *we are eager to be*.

Self-esteem means confidence in our efficacy and worth. One of the characteristics of a self-esteem deficiency, of a lack of confidence in our mind and judgment, is an excessive preoccupation with gaining the approval and avoiding the disapproval of others, hungering for validation and support at every moment of our existence. Some people dream of finding this in "romantic love." But because the problem is essentially internal, because the person does not believe in him or herself, no outside source of support can ever satisfy this hunger, except momentarily. The hunger is not for visibility; it is for self-esteem. And this cannot be supplied by others. The purpose of romantic love is, among other things, to celebrate self-esteem—not to create it in those who lack it.

Many psychologists (Harry Stack Sullivan is a striking example) regard human beings as needing the approval of others in order to approve of themselves. As popular and widespread as this viewpoint is, it is not supported by the evidence.*

---

*Granted that the support and esteem of adults can give a child an enormously valuable headstart toward successful development; still, it is demonstrable that many other factors play a role, not the least of which is the individual's own creative contribution to his or her development.

To the extent that we have successfully evolved toward autonomy (self-trust, self-reliance, self-regulation), we hope and expect that others will *perceive* our value, not *create* it. We want others to see us as we actually are—even to help us to see it more clearly— but not to invent us out of their own fantasies. To anyone in touch with reality, there is clearly no reward in such invention.

At the risk of oversimplification, one way of contrasting the mentality of the mature and autonomous individual with the (relatively) immature and dependent one is by means of the following observation. When meeting a new person, the autonomous individual tends to begin with the question, "What do I think of this person?" The immature or dependent individual tends to begin with the question, "What does this person think of me?"

As we have seen, we can feel visible in different respects and to varying degrees in different human relationships. A relationship with a casual stranger does not afford us the degree of visibility we experience with an acquaintance. A relationship with an acquaintance does not afford us the degree of visibility we experience with an intimate friend.

But there is one relationship that is unique in the depth and comprehensiveness of the visibility it entails: romantic love. In no other relationship is so much of our *self* involved. In no other relationship are as many different aspects of that self expressed. In romantic love two selves are celebrated as they are celebrated in no other context.

To appreciate fully how and why this is so, we must examine the role of sex in human existence.

Sex in Human Life

The desire for sexual as well as psychological union is one of the defining characteristics of romantic love. Yet the meaning of the sexual interaction between a man and a woman is little understood. Before placing sex in the context of romantic love, we need to make some general observations about the role of sex in human life.

It is obvious that sex is extraordinarily important to human beings. People devote a tremendous amount of time to thinking about sex, daydreaming about sex, seeing movies and reading books about sex—not to mention engaging in sex. The importance of sex in our lives is evidenced further by the fact that there is virtually no society known to us which has not laid down rules for people's sexual behavior. The most primitive tribes have rules concerning how people are to conduct themselves sexually. Certainly humankind's moral codes, especially religious codes, have been immensely preoccupied with sexual behavior. Part of the explanation for this intense concern is, of course, that sex can lead to offspring. But that is far from the only reason that social and religious codes have been concerned with controlling sexual desire and sexual expression. Some of the deeper, philosophical issues were discussed in Chapter 1.

The profound importance of sex lies in the intense pleasure it offers human beings. Pleasure, for human beings, is not a luxury, but a profound psychological need. Pleasure (in the widest sense of the term) is a metaphysical concomitant of life, the reward and consequence of successful action—just as pain is the insignia of failure, destruction, death.

In order to live, we must act, must struggle to achieve the values that sustaining life requires. It is through the state of enjoyment, through the state of happiness, through the state of pleasure that we experience the sense that life is a value, that life is worth living, worth struggling to maintain. Joy is the emotional incentive nature offers us to live. When we are successful in achieving life-enhancing values, the normal consequence is enjoyment.

Pleasure contains still another important psychological meaning. Pleasure gives us a direct experience of our own competence to deal with reality, to be successful, to achieve values—in a word, to live. Contained in the experience of pleasure, implicitly, is the feeling and thought "I am in control of my existence. I like my relationship to reality right now." Pleasure entails a sense of personal efficacy, just as pain contains a feeling of helplessness, of inefficacy, the implicit feeling and thought "I am helpless."

Sex and Self-Celebration

Pleasure, then, gives us two experiences crucial to our unfolding and development. It allows us to experience the sense that *life* is a value and to experience the sense that *we* are a value (that we are efficacious, appropriate to life, in control of our existence). There is no knowledge more important to us than that of the value of life and the value of self, and pleasure, joy, provides that knowledge, *in the vividness and intensity of direct experience.*

The intimacy and intensity of the pleasure and joy that sex potentially affords are the reason for its power in our lives. Sex is unique among pleasures in its integration of body and mind. It integrates perceptions, emotions, values, and thought. It offers us the most intense form of experience in our own total being, of experiencing our deepest and most intimate *sense of self.* Such—and this must be emphasized—is the *potential* of sex, when and to the extent that the experience is not diluted and undercut by conflict, guilt, alienation from one's partner, and so forth.

In sex, one's own person becomes a direct, immediate source, vehicle, and embodiment of pleasure. Sex offers a direct, *sensory confirmation* of the fact that happiness is possible. In sex, more than in any other activity, one experiences the fact that one is *an end in oneself* and that the purpose of life is one's own happiness. Even if the motives that lead a person to a particular sexual encounter are immature and conflicted, and even if, afterward, one is tortured by shame or guilt—so long as and to the extent that one is able to enjoy the sex act, life and one's right to the enjoyment of that life are asserting themselves within one's own being. Sex is the ultimate act of *self*-assertion.

This is true, in principle, even when there is no deep involvement with our partner. But its truth is over-poweringly apparent when sex is an expression of love. Sex is most intense when it is, simultaneously, an expression of love of self, of life, and of our partner. It is most intense because *we* then experience ourselves as most *integrated*.

Sex and Self-Awareness

In the act of sex we experience a unique and intense form of self-awareness, one generated both by the sex act itself and by the verbal-emotional-physical interaction with our partner. The nature of our self-awareness in any given experience depends on the nature of the interaction, on the degree and kind of visibility we project and, in turn, are made to feel. If and to the extent that we enjoy a strong sense of spiritual and emotional affinity with our partner, and, further, the sense of having harmoniously complementary sexual personalities, the result is the deepest possible experience of self, of being spiritually as well as physically naked, and of glorying in that fact.

Conversely, if and to the extent that we feel spiritually and/or sexually alienated and estranged from our partner, the result is that the sexual experience is felt as autistic or alienated (at best) or frustratingly "physical," or sterile and meaningless (at worst).

This does not mean that, sexually, everyone longs for romantic love and is inevitably frustrated with anything less. But it does mean that to the extent that we are alienated from our self, our sexuality, or our partner, we are cut off from the most ecstatic possibilities of sexual union.

Sex affords us the most intensely pleasurable form of self-awareness. In romantic love, when a man and a woman project that they desire to achieve this experience by means of each other's person, *that* is the highest and most intimate tribute a human being can offer or receive, *that* is the ultimate form of acknowledging the value of the person we desire and of having our own value acknowledged.

A crucial element in this experience is the perception of our efficacy as a source of pleasure to the person we love. We feel that it is our *person,* not merely our body, that is the cause of the pleasure felt by our partner. (We want to be enjoyed as more than a good sexual technician.) We feel, in effect, "Because I am what I am, I am able to cause him (or her) to feel the things he (or she) is feeling." Thus, we see our own soul, and its value, in the emotions on the face of our partner.

If sex involves an act of self-celebration, if, in sex, we desire the freedom to be spontaneous, to be emotionally open and uninhibited, to assert our right to pleasure and to flaunt our pleasure in our own being, then the person we most desire is the person with whom we feel freest to be who we are, the person who we (consciously or subconsciously) regard as our appropriate psychological mirror, the person who reflects our deepest view of our self and of life. *That is the person who will allow us to experience optimally the things we wish to experience in the realm of sex.*

Between Man and Woman

When a man and a woman encounter each other in passionate love, the factor of sex enlarges and deepens the area of desired contact between them. The longed-for "knowing" of each other is all-embracing.

We wish to explore our lover with our senses— through touch, taste, and smell. We explore and share feelings and emotions at greater length and to greater depth, and with greater regularity, than we almost ever do in any other kind of relationship. The fantasies of our partner can become the subject of our own deep, intensely personal interest. The most diverse traits, characteristics, and activities of our partner can acquire a powerful spiritual-intellectual-emotional-sexual *charge.*

The polarity of male and female generates its own dynamic tension, generates a curiosity and fascination that can be at once totally absorbed in the object and at the same time personally, intimately selfish. This is the great complement of love: that our self-interest expands to encompass our partner.

We are each of us more than simply a human being; we are a human being of a specific gender. If it is an error to overestimate the significance of this fact, it is scarcely less an error to underestimate its significance or to deny its overpowering impact on our lives.

Contained in every human being's self-concept is the awareness of being male or female. Our sexual identity is normally an integral and intimate part of our experience of personal identity. We do not experience ourselves merely as human beings, but always as a male or a female. And when a person lacks a clear sense of sexual identity, we recognize that condition as representing some failure of normal maturation.

While our sexual identity, our masculinity or femininity, is rooted in the facts of our biological nature, it does not consist of our being physically male or female; it consists of the way we psychologically *experience* our maleness or femaleness.

For example, if a man is characteristically honest in his dealings with people, this trait pertains to his psychology as a human being; it is not a sexual characteristic. If, on the other hand, he feels confident sexually, relative to women, this trait pertains to his psychology specifically as a man. If, conversely, he feels emotionally overwhelmed and inadequate at any personal encounter with a woman, we would recognize the existence of a problem in his masculinity. If a woman were to experience the penis as threatening and terrifying, we would recognize a failure of her evolution to adult femininity.

Our psychosexual identity, our sexual personality, is the product and reflection of the manner in which we learn to respond to our nature as a sexual being, just as our personal identity, in the wider sense, is a product and reflection of the manner in which we respond to our nature as a human being.

As sexual beings, there are certain questions that we necessarily confront, even if we rarely think about them consciously. To what extent am I aware of myself as a sexual entity? What is my view of sex and of its significance in human life? How do I feel about my own body? (This last does not mean: How do I appraise my body aesthetically? But rather: Is my body experienced as a value, as a source of pleasure?) How do I view the opposite sex? How do I feel about the body of the opposite sex? How do I feel about the sexual encounter of male and female? What is the level of my ability to act and respond freely in this encounter? It is our implicit answers to such questions that underlie our sexual psychology.

It need hardly be said that our attitude toward these issues is not formed in a psychological vacuum. On the contrary: in sex, perhaps more than in any other realm, the total of our personality tends to find expression. More than one study has suggested that, other things being equal, the higher the level of our general self-esteem, the more likely it is that we will respond healthily and affirmatively to the fact of our own sexuality and to the phenomenon of sex in general.

Since our sexuality is an inherent part of our humanness, a mature, well-evolved individual experiences his or her sexuality as integrated into his or her total being—and experiences the sex act as a natural expression of that being. To be integrated with our sexuality is indispensable for fulfillment in romantic love.

A healthy masculinity or femininity is the consequence or expression of an affirmative response to our sexual nature. This entails a strong, enthusiastic awareness of our own sexuality; a positive (fearless and guiltless) response to the phenomenon of sex; a disposition to experience sex as an *expression* of the self, rather than as something alien, darkly incomprehensible, sinful, or "dirty"; a positive and self-valuing response to one's own body; an enthusiastic appreciation of the body of the opposite sex; a capacity for freedom, spontaneity, and delight in the sexual encounter.

Many years ago, while running a therapy group, I listened to a number of clients talk about the varied notions of masculinity and femininity upheld at different times and in different cultures. One of the clients asked me what personal meaning I found in the concepts of masculinity and femininity. I answered, more or less spontaneously, that masculinity was the expression of a man's belief that the creation of woman was nature's most brilliant idea, and that femininity was the expression of a woman's belief that the creation of man was nature's most brilliant idea! Doubtless that formulation lacked something in scientific elegance; nonetheless, I am not at all confident that I can do better now.*

In any case, what is easy enough to see is the enormous pleasure that a man can know in the experience of himself as male, as the inhabitant of a male body, and the enormous pleasure a woman can know in the experience of herself as female, as the inhabitant of a female body—and the unutterable joy of encountering the body and the person of the other, the encounter of man with woman, of woman with man, and the discovery, through passion and intimacy, that "the other" is, in fact, *the other side of oneself.*

Just as our sexual personality is essential to our sense of who we are, so it is essential to that which we wish to objectify and to see reflected or made visible in human relationships. The experience of *full visibility* and *full self-objectification* entails being perceived,

---

*Of course, each one of us carries within our psyche a variety of connotations and associations attached to the terms "masculine" and "feminine." These personal meanings reflect events in our individual life history, male and female models who may have inspired us, different viewpoints prevalent in our culture, whatever thinking we ourselves may have done on the subject, and, last but far from least, biological forces deep within our organism that speak to us in a wordless language we have barely begun to decipher.

and perceiving our self not merely as a certain kind of human being, but as a certain kind of man or woman.

In point of fact, we want both: to be perceived as a certain kind of human being *and* a certain kind of man or woman.

A man may wish to have his strength perceived by the woman in his life; he may also wish her to perceive his sensitivity, his vulnerability, his need from time to time *not* to be fully "responsible" and "in control," and also to have it understood that there is no conflict or contradiction among these various facets of who he is. A woman may wish to have her sensitivity and intuitiveness appreciated; she may also wish her man to appreciate her strength and aggressiveness, and to have him understand that no conflict or contradiction is involved.

The optimal experience of visibility and self-objectification requires interaction with a member of the opposite sex. We all carry male and female aspects within us; but in man, the male principle ordinarily predominates; in woman, the female principle predominates. In relating to the opposite sex, we are permitted to experience the full range of who we are. *The polarity between man and woman generates and accentuates this awareness.*

Of course, there are aspects of this ability which are best achieved with members of one's own sex. A man knows what it feels like to be a man in a way no woman can know; a woman knows what it feels like to be a woman in a way no man can know. But a *wider range of possibilities* can be explored between members of the opposite sex. Such a relationship represents a vaster keyboard on which *more notes can be hit* and a richer music can be created.

A member of the opposite sex, with whom we enjoy a strong mutuality of mind and values, many fundamental affinities, as well as complementary differences, is capable of perceiving and personally responding to us both as a human being and as a sexual being. The unique, gender-induced perspective of man and woman, in confronting the opposite sex, represents, at least potentially, the fullest possible range of "knowing" the other.

I shall not attempt to deal, in the context of this book, with the difficult and complex question of homosexuality and bisexuality. Obviously the entire context of this work is heterosexual; we deal with the model of man/woman relationships, even though much of what is said clearly applies to homosexual love relationships. If one regards homosexuality or bisexuality as representing fully as mature a level of development as heterosexuality, some of the preceding observations will be unacceptable. If, on the other hand, one takes the view, as I do, not that homosexuality or bisexuality are "immoral" or "wrong" or should be illegal, but that they generally do reflect a detour or blockage on the pathway to full maturity as an adult human being, then my reasoning will have, I believe, more persuasiveness. To say more would take me farther afield than I care to go.

To be sexually desired, in the context of romantic love, although not necessarily in the context of more casual relationships, is to be seen and wanted for what one is as a person, including what one is as a man or a woman. The essence of the romantic love response is: "I see you as a person, and because you are what you are, I love and desire you, for my happiness in general and my sexual happiness in particular."

Our spiritual-emotional-sexual response to our partner is a consequence of seeing him or her as the embodiment of our highest values, and as being crucially important to our personal happiness. "Highest," in this context, does not necessarily mean noblest or most exalted; it means most important, in terms of our personal needs and desires and in terms of what we wish to find and experience in life. As an integral part of that response, we see the loved object as being crucially important to our *sexual* happiness. The needs of our spirit and of our body melt into each other; we experience our most enraptured sense of *wholeness*.

The Romantic-Love Response

Looking back at the road we have traveled, we can appreciate some of the basic needs to which romantic love can respond.

There is the simple need for companionship. There is the need to love, and to admire. There is the need to be loved, and to feel visible. There is the need of self-discovery. There is the need of sexual fulfillment. There is the need of fully experiencing oneself as a man or as a woman.

And as our journey continues, we will see that still other needs inspire a longing for romantic love. There is the need for a private universe, a refuge from the struggles of the world, that romantic love has a unique power to fulfill. There is the need to share our excitement in being alive—and to enjoy and be nourished by the excitement of another.

These things are called "needs," not because we will necessarily die without them, but because they make so enormous a contribution to our well-being, to our continued efficacious functioning. They have *survival value*.

Ordinarily we do not reflect on the needs we seek to satisfy through romantic love. We merely feel them; we do not conceptualize them. The practical value of doing so is not only that it helps us to understand the nature of love but also because we thereby provide ourselves with criteria by which to assess our relationships. If, for example, we notice that we do not feel visible in a relationship with someone who professes to love us and whom we profess to love, we can recognize more clearly that something is amiss—*if we are aware of the importance of feeling visible*. We shall pick up this theme in Chapter 4.

We cannot fully understand the roots of romantic

love without considering the particular factors that inspire us to fall in love with one human being rather than another. We need to consider the selection process involved in "falling in love." To this subject we shall now turn.

THREE

•

Choice in Romantic Love

Prologue: The Shock of Recognition

In a joyful relationship between a man and a woman, the experience of love, desire, and pleasure does not flow along a simple, unidirectional pathway, but rather flows through a reciprocal cycle of continuing mutual reinforcement. Loving an individual, we perceive him or her as a source of real or potential happiness; desire is born; desire generates actions that result in pleasure or joy, through involvement with the loved person; pleasure operates through a kind of feedback loop to intensify desire and love; and so on. In this manner love develops and strengthens.

Fascination, attraction, passion may be born "at first sight." Love is not. Love requires knowledge, and knowledge requires time. People sometimes speak of "falling in love at first sight," because that is how it can *seem* in retrospect, when the powerful emotional response of the first moment is validated and confirmed by later experiences in such a way that love does indeed evolve.

Still, in the early stages of a new relationship, and sometimes even in the first moment of meeting, it is not uncommon for future lovers to experience a sudden "shock of recognition," an odd sense of familiarity, a sense of encountering a person already known on some level and in some mysterious, seemingly inexplicable, way. There is a fascination with the strangeness of "the other," true enough, but there is also, very often, almost the opposite, the sense of something subtly and powerfully *known,* as if they were encountering the concretization of something formerly existing as potential within their own psyche. With a shock of recognition they see this "other" who is at the same time *not* "an other."

We need to understand what ignites this initial attraction and what is the foundation of the bond that forms. I spoke earlier of passionate love resting on some significant "mutuality of mind and values." That is a very wide abstraction. It is necessary to consider, specifically, what it entails, and how it is manifested, and how it can possibly be recognized, sometimes, in the very first moments of a new encounter. The answers will help illuminate why we fall in love with one person rather than another.

Sense of Life

There is one concept that is essential to an understanding of romantic love and the selection process: "sense of life." Romantic love entails, at its core, a profound and shared sense of life.

A sense of life is the emotional form in which we experience our deepest view of existence and our relationship to existence. It is, in effect, the emotional corollary of a metaphysics—of a *personal* metaphysics, one might say—reflecting the subconsciously held sum of our broadest and deepest attitudes and conclusions concerning the world, life, and ourselves.

Our sense of life can reflect a strong and healthy self-esteem and an undiluted sense of the value of existence, a conviction that the universe is open to the efficacy of our thought and effort. Or it can reflect the torture of self-doubt and the anxiety of feeling that we live in a universe that is unintelligible and hostile. It can reflect a view of life as exultation or a view of life as sordid senselessness. It can embody eagerness and self-confidence, or self-doubt and embittered resentment, or muted, wistful longing, or anguished, tragic defiance, or gentle, uncomplaining resignation, or aggressive impotence, or wilfully perverse martyrdom— or almost any combination of these attitudes, mixed in varying proportions and degrees.

The formation of our sense of life begins in early childhood, long before we are able to think about the world and the self in conceptual terms. In the course of evolution from childhood, we inevitably encounter certain fundamental facts of reality, facts about the nature of existence and the nature of human life to which we can respond in a variety of ways and with varying degrees of realism and appropriateness. It is the cumulative sum of these responses that constitutes our distinctive sense of life. Later, adult observations and learning obviously affect our attitudes in these matters to some extent; but to a profound degree, attitudes formed early in life, ahead of a great deal of "hard" information, prove remarkably tenacious and resistant to change.

To begin with a basic example, it is an inescapable fact of reality that *consciousness* and *purposefully directed awareness* are necessities of our existence, that is, that we require knowledge and the acquisition of knowledge requires the effort of conceptual thought. The position a young person progressively develops regarding this issue is not arrived at by explicit decision; it is not a matter of a single choice. It is arrived at by the cumulative implication of a long series of choices and responses in the face of specific situations involving the need to think and to expand the range of awareness. We are not concerned, in this immediate context, with the question of all the factors that contribute to the kind of pattern that will be established, but only with the fact that a *pattern is established*.

Depending on many factors, we may learn to respond positively and joyfully, learning to take an active pleasure in the exercise of our mind. Or we may learn to approach intellectual effort grudgingly and dutifully, viewing it, in effect, as a "necessary evil." Or we may come to regard mental effort with lethargic resentment or fear, viewing it as an unfair burden and an imposition, and determining to avoid it whenever possible.

What gradually forms and hardens in our psychology over time is a trend, a policy, a habit—a position or a premise *by implication*. It is in this manner that all sense-of-life attitudes are formed.

A great many issues are involved in an individual's sense of life, and I shall indicate only a few fundamentals:

It is a fact of reality that human beings are neither omniscient nor infallible. We discover, very early, not only that knowledge must be acquired by a process of directed awareness, but that there is no guarantee, in any given case, that our effort will necessarily and automatically be successful. We may learn to accept the responsibility of thought and judgment willingly, realistically, and more or less fearlessly, prepared to bear the consequences of our conclusions and subsequent actions, recognizing that no reasonable alternative to this policy exists. Or we may learn to react with fear and with a longing to escape responsibility, by shrinking the area of awareness, thought, and action so as to minimize the "risk" entailed by possible errors and/or by passing to others the responsibility we have come to dread, living, in effect, off their thoughts, their judgments, their values, their conclusions.

If two people meet who have responded to this challenge in radically opposing ways, a gulf exists between them that constitutes a formidable barrier to the initiation of romantic love.

It is a fact of reality that we human beings must live long-range, that we must project our goals into the future and work to achieve them, and that this demands of us the ability and willingness, when and if necessary, to defer immediate pleasures and to endure unavoidable frustrations. Even the simplest manner of existence demands of us that we give some thought to the consequences of our actions; we cannot escape the reality that there will be a tomorrow. (The error of those who live "only in the future," at the cost of denying the present, is a different issue, unrelated to our immediate point.) We may learn to accept that there is a tomorrow, that actions do have consequences, and we may look at these facts of life realistically and unself-pityingly, preserving our ambition for values. Or we may rebel in resentment against a universe that does not grant instant fulfillment to all desires, stamping our foot at reality, in effect, and seek only the sort of values that can be attained easily and swiftly.

It is a fact of reality that, in the course of a lifetime, a human being will inevitably experience some degree of suffering as well as witnessing some degree; the degree may be great or small. What is not inevitable, however, is the status that we will ascribe to suffering, that is, the significance that we will attach to it in our life and in our view of existence. We may preserve a relatively unclouded sense of the value of existence, no matter what adversity or suffering is encountered; we may preserve the conviction that happiness and success are normal and natural and that pain, defeat, disaster, and disappointment are the abnormal and the accidental (just as we view health, not disease, as our normal state). Or we may decide that suffering and defeat are the very essence of existence, that happiness and success are the temporary, abnormal, and accidental.

It is in the nature of a living organism that it must act to preserve its own life and well-being. It is in the distinctive nature of human organisms that we must *choose* to value our own life and happiness sufficiently to generate the consciousness, thought, effort, and action they require. For us, as human beings, the process is not automatic; we are not biologically "wired" to make the right choice, the choice that in fact serves our well-being. We may develop the life-assertive self-respect appropriate to a living being and may form a solemn ambition to experience happiness, as unswerving loyalty to our own values, a proud refusal to treat them as an object of renunciation or sacrifice. Or, fearing the effort, the responsibility, the integrity, the courage that such rational selfishness and self-value require, we may begin the process of giving up our soul before it is even fully formed, surrendering aspirations, surrendering happiness, surrendering values, not to some tangible beneficiary but to a nameless, unidentified lethargy or apprehension.

Our sense of life is of crucial importance in the formation of our basic values, since all value choices rest on an implicit view of the being who values and of the world in which such a being must act. Our sense of life underlies all other feelings, all emotional responses —like the leitmotiv of a soul, the basic theme of a personality. *This* is the relevance of sense of life to romantic love. A "soulmate" is one who shares, in important respects, our sense of life.

When we encounter another human being, we feel the presence of that music within him or her. We sense how that individual experiences him- or herself, the joyfulness, or fearfulness, or defensiveness of his or her approach to life. We sense the level of excitement or the level of deadness, and our body and emotions respond faster than thought can take shape in words.

In romantic relationships, the affirmative response of each party to the sense of life of the other—which can sometimes happen in the first moment of meeting—is crucial to the experience of love and to the projection of mutual visibility. It is often the factor that ignites the relationship. In romantic love, we feel implicitly, "My lover sees life as I do. He (or she) faces existence as I face it. He (or she) experiences the fact of being alive as I experience it."

In my Intensive on *Self-Esteem and Romantic Relationships,* I take my students through an exercise, the purpose of which is to make them aware of how much we know about one another, how much we almost instantly sense and respond to, often without conscious and explicit recognition. Everyone in the room is asked to sit on the floor facing a total stranger and sit quietly looking at the person opposite, without words, without moving, just looking, just absorbing the being of the other person, allowing impressions to form, allowing fantasies concerning the other person to develop without censorship, to imagine what this person was like as a child, what this person might be like as a lover or companion, to imagine what kind of conflicts or struggles this person may have, to imagine how this person feels about him- or herself, and so forth. Then, after a few moments of silence, one person speaks, sharing thoughts, fantasies, and impressions, while the other listens silently, neither agreeing nor disagreeing, neither confirming nor disconfirming. Then the process is reversed; the person who has spoken is now silent and the one who has been silent now speaks, sharing impressions and fantasies concerning the partner. Then they are asked to comment and to name what they feel their partner was right or wrong about. At this point there is almost always great astonishment and great excitement in the room; the accuracy rate is very high; people are exhilarated and sometimes amazed at how sensitive they are, how much they know, how much they can see. Most of them had not been aware of it.

Among the many ways in which a sense of life is communicated, perhaps the rarest is by explicit, conceptual statement. Of course, as a relationship progresses, knowledge begins to arrive in more recognizable forms: two people discover their affinity by learning of each other's values and disvalues, for instance—by observing each other's manner of talking, of smiling, of standing, of moving, of expressing emotions, of reacting to events, and so forth. They discover it by the way they react to each other, by the things said and by the things not said, by the explanations it is not necessary to give, by sudden, unexpected signs of mutual understanding. Virtually everyone has had this experience.

Sometimes, one of the most eloquent signs of a

sense-of-life affinity is common likes and dislikes in the field of art. Art is a sense-of-life realm, more explicitly than any other human activity. And an individual's sense of life is crucial to determining personal artistic responses.

Two individuals' discussion of their respective ideas is not unimportant; it can be very important, indeed. This obvious fact should not be denied or overlooked. But mere abstract, intellectual agreement on particular subjects is not sufficient by itself to establish an authentic sense-of-life affinity. In fact, such agreement can be misleading; it can create the delusion for the two parties that they have more in common than they actually have. I have seen a number of young people mistakenly marry because they assumed that wide areas of philosophical agreement were a sufficient foundation for an intimate relationship; they were oblivious to the deeper sense-of-life differences that divided them.

Without a significant sense-of-life affinity, no broad, fundamental, and intimate experience of visibility is possible. We may be admired for some particular quality or qualities, by a person with an alien sense of life, but our feeling of gratification, if any, would be extremely limited; we would sense that the other person was admiring us for the wrong reasons.

I am thinking, for example, of a man with a self-confident, affirmative sense of life, engaged in a difficult and challenging pursuit, who was admired by a woman whose own sense of life was defiantly tragic, so that the admiration she projected was for the image of a heroic but doomed martyr. The man who was the recipient of this admiration did not feel gratifyingly visible, because the image clashed with his own non-tragic sense of life.

In romantic love, optimally experienced, we are admired for the things we wish to be admired for, and— equally important—in a way and from a perspective that is in accord with our own view of life. So here, in this area of vital similarities, we have the essential foundation of passionate and sustained romantic attraction. *We are drawn to consciousnesses like our own.*

But our picture, if we stopped here, would be incomplete. It is not a literal mirror-image of ourselves that we are seeking. The *foundation* of a relationship lies in basic similarities. The *excitement* of a relationship lies, to an important extent, in complementary differences. The two together constitute the context in which romantic love is born.

Complementary Differences

The principle of basic similarities and complementary differences can be observed, on the most fundamental level, in the ultimate ground of attraction between man and woman. On the most abstract plane, the affinity, the basic similarity, without which love could not happen, is the fact that they are both *human*. The complementary difference that lends unique excitement to the encounter is the fact of being *male* and *female*.

On a more specific plane, when we encounter another person who has learned survival strategies similar to our own, whose manner of being-in-the-world is one we recognize intimately, whose coping and adapting processes resemble those that we ourselves have acquired, there is the shock of recognition, the sense of a profound bond—and this is, in effect, the base or foundation that supports the structure of a relationship. Without it, serious, mature love between man and woman does not develop. But no two human beings are literally the same; no two people develop in an identical manner; no two actualize (make real through action) exactly the same potentials. Just as there is specialization in labor, so there is specialization in personality development.

To illustrate: One person actualizes more of his or her verbal-intellectual skills than another; another individual moves more in the direction of the development of the intuitive function. One person is predominately action oriented; another is more contemplative. One person is more artistically inclined; another is more "worldly." One person is inclined to have a strong attachment to the past; another lives almost entirely in the present; another seems to live predominately in the future. One person may be oriented almost exclusively toward achievements in the area of work; another with the developing and nurturing of relationships. One person may be deeply in love with the physical aspects of existence; another with the intellectual; another with the spiritual. We possess these potentials to different degrees, and we actualize them to different degrees. All of these possibilities exist, to some extent, in all of us, but the formula of the precise combination for any of us is as unique and individual as a set of fingerprints.

We are most likely to fall in love with that person in relationship to whom we experience, simultaneously, basic affinities and complementary differences. When a man and a woman experience differences as complementary, they experience them as stimulating, challenging, exciting—a dynamic force that enhances feelings of aliveness, expansion, growth.

Clearly not all differences between people are complementary; some may be antagonistic. It is a superficial oversimplification to conclude, as some psychologists have suggested, that "opposites attract." It is at least equally true to observe that "opposites repel." There are men and women whose cognitive styles (way of thinking and of processing experience), whose way of relating to time, to action, and to the world are so different that little can exist between them but friction, impatience, and irritability, particularly if they attempt intimacy.

For the successful intimacy inherent in romantic love, a man and a woman must experience their differences as mutually enriching, as capable of drawing out untapped potentials in each other, so that their encounter is an adventure in expanded consciousness and expanded aliveness.

Two people, one whose dominant cognitive style is verbal-intellectual, the other whose dominant cognitive style is intuitive, may have an enriching and stimulating relationship if each respects and appreciates the cognitive style of the other. But if each regards the other's cognitive style as antagonistic, conflict and dissonance necessarily result.

Or again, whether a person who is predominately action oriented and a person who is predominately spiritually oriented experience their differences as complementary or antagonistic depends, to an important extent, on the willingness and ability of each to appreciate and find value in the orientation of the other. This in turn depends, to an important extent, on the ability and willingness of each to accept and respect that latent or subdominant element within him- or herself.

Let us pause for a moment on this last point. Often, we are most intolerant toward others who have those very traits or possibilities that we have disowned in ourselves. I know a woman who has disowned her own aggressiveness and is often angered by that trait in her lover. I know a man who has disowned his own sensitivity and who is typically impatient with that trait in a woman. Often husbands and wives fight about and complain of in each other the very traits they themselves possess and do not wish to know about. I am thinking, for example, of a man who could tolerate virtually any feeling in himself except helplessness, and when his wife displayed that feeling he became angry with her. He did not know that he valued the fact that she occasionally allowed herself to feel helpless, that she was, in effect, carrying that state for both of them. I once worked with a very active, very ambitious woman who, while she occasionally complained about her husband's passivity, actually valued that very quality in him; through him, she allowed herself to experience it vicariously, almost like a secret luxury not to be permitted to herself directly.

Romantic love often coexists with just such frictions

as I am describing; every day, couples who experience some differences as complementary and some as antagonistic fall genuinely in love. The point is that often conflict can be resolved by recognizing and owning in ourselves just those traits and characteristics that sometimes frustrate or annoy us in those we love; learning to accept those traits in ourselves, we are better able to accept them in others.

Complementary differences between partners who accept themselves and each other can be a powerful source for the stimulation of growth and enhanced self-discovery. Each represents to the other a doorway into new worlds. The firmer the self-esteem of the participants, the more likely this is to occur; they are less inclined to perceive differences as threatening.

Sometimes we see in another human being the embodiment of a part of our self that has been struggling to emerge. If that other person sees a similar possibility in us, an explosion of love can take place, the sense of an excitingly increased experience of aliveness through contact, involvement, and interaction.

In fact, one way to gain deeper insight into a love relationship is to ask ourselves: *What parts of myself does my lover bring me into fresh contact with? How do I experience myself in this relationship? What feels most alive within me in the presence of this person?* In answering these questions, we can come to appreciate some of the most important reasons why we have fallen in love with a particular person.

I want to introduce one clarification before proceeding. Differences can be complementary and can contribute to the success of a relationship only when the traits of each individual are valuable and desirable. Values and disvalues are *not* "complementary." We do not see a passionate love affair between a person with a high self-esteem and a person with a low self-esteem, nor between a highly intelligent person and one who is aggressively stupid. Such differences are inherently antagonistic, not mutually stimulating. In order for differences to be complementary, rather than antagonistic,

You are cordially invited...

...to join Dr. Nathaniel Branden at his Intensive Workshops on Self-Esteem, Man/Woman Relationships, and Personal Transformation, offered throughout the United States.

For free information about Dr. Branden's Intensives, tape cassettes, and books, return this postage-paid card.

NAME _____

ADDRESS _____

CITY _____ STATE _____ ZIP _____

PHONE (evenings) _____

BUSINESS REPLY CARD

FIRST CLASS PERMIT NO. 4596   BEVERLY HILLS, CA.

POSTAGE WILL BE PAID BY ADDRESSEE

THE BIOCENTRIC INSTITUTE
P.O. BOX 4009
BEVERLY HILLS, CA. 90213

NO POSTAGE
NECESSARY
IF MAILED
IN THE
UNITED STATES

they must fall within the realm of that which is *optional*. They cannot pertain to the fundamentals of existence. The difference between self-esteem and self-hatred, or between honesty and dishonesty, is not "optional." They do not represent equally valid orientations or states of being. The differences are fundamental. And in such fundamentals, we desire affinity. In matters such as cognitive or personality style, we can welcome and enjoy differences, within a certain range, because here differences can be equally valuable.

It sometimes happens that a dishonest person is attracted to the honesty of another, just as an insecure person can be attracted to the self-esteem of another, seeking that which one lacks in oneself. But the attraction is unilateral, not reciprocal. Honesty is not attracted by dishonesty, self-esteem is not attracted by self-doubt. The foundation for mutual love does not exist.

When the foundation of a mutual love does exist, when there is an appropriate combination of basic affinities and complementary differences between a man and a woman, and, further, if they are in a position to be available to love at that point in their lives, love begins to develop long before the couple can articulate many of the grounds of their mutual attraction. The experience of many men and women who have been together for years is that they keep discovering new reasons for being in love, reasons that were intuitively or subconsciously grasped very early but that needed a long time to find their way into words. Not that anyone ever names *all* the reasons and not that it is necessary to do so. But for couples who wish to explore this territory, it is useful to ask: *In what ways are we alike? In what ways—that we enjoy and are stimulated by—are we different?*

Perhaps I should mention that the mere enumeration of another person's traits will never be completely satisfying. There is always the matter of the way those traits interact within the particular personality, the degree to which the various traits exist, and the balance among them. "Balance" and "degree" are key issues. For instance, I have always enjoyed the presence of a certain amount of "male" in the personality of women I have cared for. But obviously there is a world of difference between a woman who is totally integrated with her femininity and at the same time possesses an element of "male" in her makeup and a woman whose "male" element is so powerful that one has to remind oneself that she is a woman. I have always felt that women totally devoid of any "male" principle are very uninteresting as women; and many women have shared with me the feeling that a man totally devoid of any "female" in his personality is equally unexciting. But the question of degree is obviously of the greatest importance.

Thus far, in addressing ourselves to the question of why we fall in love with one person rather than another, we have been operating more or less implicitly on the assumption of mature, romantic love. But the principle of basic affinities and complementary differences applies equally in immature love relationships. In view of how statistically common such relationships are, it seems desirable to say a few words about them so as to illuminate further the principle we have been exploring and to appreciate in what way immature love differs from the concept of romantic love presented in this book.

Immature Love

"Maturity" and "immaturity" are concepts that refer to the success or failure of an individual's biological, intellectual, and psychological evolution to an adult stage of development.

In mature love relationships, "complementary differences" refers, predominately, to complementary *strengths*. In immature relationships, "complementary differences" tends to refer to complementary *weaknesses*. These weaknesses include needs, wants, and other personality traits that reflect some failure of healthy development, some failure of psychological maturation. As we shall see, we deal here, most essentially, with the issue of separation and individuation, with an individual's success or failure at the task of reaching an adult level of autonomy.

Many a person faces life with an attitude that, if translated into explicit speech, which it almost never is, would amount to the declaration, "When I was five years old, important needs of mine were not met—and until they are, I'm not moving on to six!" On a basic level these people are very passive, even though, on more superficial levels, they may sometimes appear active and "aggressive." At bottom, they are waiting, waiting to be rescued, waiting to be told they are good boys or good girls, waiting to be validated or confirmed by some outside source.

So their whole lives may be organized around the desire to please, to be taken care of, or, alternatively, to control and dominate, to manipulate and *coerce* the satisfaction of their needs and wants, because they don't trust the authenticity of anyone's love or caring. They have no confidence that what they are, without their facades and manipulations, is *enough*.

Whether their act is to be helpless and dependent, or to be controlling, overprotective, "responsible," "grown-up," there is an underlying sense of inadequacy, of nameless deficiency, that they feel only other human beings can correct. They are alienated from their own internal sources of strength and support; they are alienated from their own powers.

Whether they seek completion and fulfillment through domination or submission, through controlling or being controlled, through ordering or obeying, there is the same fundamental sense of emptiness, a void in the center of their being, a screaming hole where an autonomous self failed to develop. They have never assimilated and integrated the basic fact of human aloneness; individuation has not been attained to a level appropriate to their chronological development.

They have failed to transfer the source of their

approval from others to self. They have failed to evolve into a state of self-responsibility. They have failed to make peace with the immutable fact of their ultimate aloneness—therefore they are crippled in their efforts to relate.

They view other human beings with suspicion, hostility, and feelings of alienation, or else see them as life belts by which they can stay afloat in the stormy sea of their own anxiety and insecurity. There is a tendency for immature persons to view others primarily, if not exclusively, as sources for the gratification of their own wants and needs, not as human beings in their own right, much as an infant views a parent. So their relationships tend to be dependent and manipulative, not the encounter of two autonomous selves who feel free to express themselves honestly and are able to appreciate and enjoy each other's being, but the encounter of two incomplete beings who look to love to solve the problem of their internal deficiencies, to finish magically the unfinished business of childhood, to fill up the holes in their personality, to make of "love" a substitute for evolution to maturity and self-responsibility.

These are some of the "basic similarities" shared by immature persons who fall in love. To understand why immature love is born is also to understand why it generally dies so swiftly.

An immature woman looks at her lover and, deep in her psyche, there is the thought, "My father made me feel rejected; you will take his place and give me what he failed to give me. I will create a house for you, and cook your meals, and bear your children—I will be your good little girl."

Or a woman experiences herself as unloved or rejected by one or both parents. She fails to acknowledge the magnitude of her hurt and self-deprecatory feelings, and she passes into the *semblance* of adulthood. But the sense of unfinished business, the sense of incompleteness as a person, remains and continues to play a role in her motivation, beneath the surface of awareness. She "falls in love" with a man who, whatever his other virtues, shares important characteristics with her rejecting parent(s). Perhaps he is cold, unemotional, unable or unwilling to express love. Like a losing gambler who cannot resist returning to the table where past defeats were suffered, she feels compulsively drawn to him. *This time she will not lose.* She will melt him. She will find a way to melt him. She will find a way to inspire in him all the responses she longed for and failed to receive as a child. And in so doing, she feels, she will redeem her childhood—she will win the victory over her past.

What she does not realize is that, unless other factors intervene to generate a positive change in her psychology, the man is useful to her, is serviceable to her, in the drama she is playing only so long as he remains somewhat aloof, somewhat uncaring, somewhat distant from her. If he would become warm and loving, he no longer would be a suitable understudy for Mother or Father; he would no longer be appropriate for the role in which she has cast him. So at the same time that she cries for love, she takes careful measures to maintain the distance between them to prevent him from giving her the very things she asks for. If, somehow, in spite of her efforts, he does become loving and caring, the likelihood is that she will feel disoriented and will withdraw; probably she will fall out of love with him. "Why?" she cries to her psychotherapist, "do I always fall for men who don't know how to love?"

A man looks at his bride and there is the thought, "Now I am a married man; I am grown up; I have responsibilities—just like Father. I will work hard, I will be your protector, I will take care of you—just as Father did with Mother. Then he—and you—and everyone—will see that I am a good boy."

Or, when a man is a little boy his mother deserts her family to go off with her lover. The little boy feels betrayed and abandoned; it is *he* Mother has left, not Father. (This is the natural egocentricity of childhood.) He tells himself—perhaps with Father's help and encouragement—that "women are like that, not to be trusted." He resolves never to be vulnerable to such pain again. No woman will ever be allowed to make him suffer as Mother did. But years later he knows only two kinds of relationships with women: those in which he cares a good deal less than the woman, and it is he who hurts and betrays her; and those in which he has selected a woman who inevitably will not remain true to him, inevitably will make him suffer. Sooner or later, he almost always ends up with the second kind of woman—to complete the unfinished business of childhood (which he can never complete successfully in this manner, *because the woman is not his mother,* she is only a symbolic substitute). When the woman "lets him down," he professes to be shocked and bewildered. The intense "love affairs" of his life are of this second kind. He is disconnected from the original pain, from the source of the problem, from the feelings he disowned long ago; therefore he is powerless to deal with them effectively and to resolve them; he is the prisoner of that which he has failed to confront; but deep in his psyche, without a solution's ever being found, the drama continues. *Next* time he will beat the table. Meanwhile, for consolation, for rest, for recreation, for revenge, let him hurt as many women as he can. He asks, "Is romantic love a delusion? It never seems to work for me."

I have developed an exercise for my Intensive on *Self-Esteem and Romantic Relationships* that bears on this issue. The group is given the following instructions: "Take your notebooks and at the top of a fresh page write *Mother.* Then write six or eight phrases or words that would describe or characterize her. Then write a sentence about how you perceive her ability to give and receive love. Now go to a new page, write *Father* at the top, and make the same kind of list for him. Now turn to a new page and write *One of the ways I felt frustrated by Mother or Father was___* and then write six or eight different endings for that sentence. Now, on a fresh page, write the name of either your spouse in your first marriage or the person with whom you have had the most painfully intense love affair of your life. And below that name write six or eight phrases or words to describe or characterize that person, again ending with a statement on how you perceive the person's ability to give and receive love. Now turn to a new page and write *One of the ways I felt frustrated by* (fill in the person's name)—and then write six or eight endings to that sentence." Invariably one hears groans, laughter, and curses throughout the room. "My God," someone cries, "I married my mother!" Someone else shouts back, *"I* married my father!" "At least I had the sense not to get married," someone else exclaims. For many, the implications of those five pages are truly shocking . . . and yet not entirely shocking.

On one level, it is true enough to say that a characteristic of immature love is that the man or woman does not perceive his or her partner realistically; fantasies and projections take the place of clear vision. And yet, on a deeper level, on a level not ordinarily acknowledged, there is awareness, there is recognition, there is knowledge of whom they have chosen. They are not, in fact, blind; but the game in which they are engaged may require that they pretend, to themselves, to be blind. This allows them to go through the motions of being bewildered, hurt, outraged, shocked, when their partner behaves precisely as their own life scenario requires. Evidence for this lies in the consistency with which immature persons find precisely those immature other persons whose problems and style of being will complement and mesh with their own.

A woman, for example, who experiences a need to suffer, to be "second" in relationships, to reassure Mother that she is not a competitor, will manage, with the accuracy of a guided missile, to find and fall in love with a married man who, however devoted to her he may profess to be, absolutely "cannot" leave his wife.

A man who experiences a need to play at being strong, protective, responsible, "in control," will find a woman who experiences a need to play at being weak, helpless, dependent, childlike. Out of such "complementary differences," sometimes, "love" ignites.

There are females who feel comfortable in the role of mother and child but not woman. There are males who feel comfortable in the role of father and child but not man. "Across a crowded room"—or in the midst of multitudes—they manage to find each other. Then they alternate roles, protector and helpless one, moving back and forth, switching, guided by an exchange of unspoken signals, each providing for the other a stage on which to act out the drama of their immaturity, of their unfinished business from childhood, and at the same time pretending they are adults.

Always we can observe the basic affinity—the insecurity, the role-playing, the commitment to an unreal existence—as well as the complementary differences— the different but complementary acts, masks, roles, games, that allow each to have the experience of having encountered a soulmate.

Even though these relationships tend to be unstable, tend not to last, tend to explode or wear out, there are times, there are moments, when they offer excitement, a heightened sense of awareness, a heightened sense of aliveness, even a sense of magic.

Such relationships sometimes exhibit all the characteristics of an addiction. The self-esteem of the participants is so tied to the support and validation of the partner that even the briefest absences, even the briefest separations, can trigger anxiety, can trigger panic, can trigger despair. And, even when such a relationship ends, the one who is left may experience all the "withdrawal symptoms" of an addict whose supply of heroin has been terminated. (See Peele and Brodsky, *Love and Addiction,* 1975.)

The difference between mature romantic love and an immature love that may call itself "romantic" will be elaborated further in Chapter 4. Especially relevant will be our discussion of self-esteem and autonomy. But for the moment we need to remember that when we speak of "maturity" and "immaturity" we are dealing always with a matter of degree. It is convenient, when we wish to isolate a principle, to characterize individuals and relationships as "mature" or "immature." At the same time we recognize that in reality these concepts operate along a continuum. I make this point at this moment because, having read the description of immature love, the reader may feel confused, sensing that his or her own relationship is mature in some respects and immature in others and wondering how to categorize it. The truth is that just as a given individual may function maturely in some respects but not in others, so a given relationship may be mature in some respects but not in others.

Furthermore, we need to recognize that a highly evolved, mature man or woman may still have moments of "immaturity," feelings and responses that are far below the general level of his or her functioning. But such moments tend to be accepted by such persons for what they are: they do not become the occasion for self-blame or self-condemnation. It is not the case that a mature man or woman never feels the desire or inclination to be a child, to be helpless, to be irresponsible. Rather, if circumstances permit, he or she allows such feelings, accepts them, owns them, but does not get stuck there, does not remain fixated there for life. The decision to flow with such feelings and to act on them when it is safe and appropriate to do so involves a choice, not a compulsion.

A mature man or woman accepts occasional immature feelings as normal and even pleasurable. An immature man or woman disowns such feelings and remains imprisoned by them.*

---

*I discuss the process by which we remain trapped within feelings and emotions we deny and disown in my book *The Disowned Self*.

A Curious Variable: Rhythm and Energy

Before concluding our discussion of the selection process in romantic love, there is one variable that needs to be mentioned which I have reserved for separate comment, a variable that can be deeply significant for whether or not love actually ignites between a man and a woman and yet is almost never recognized or understood. Its impact upon a potential relationship, whether positive or negative, can be very powerful, yet very subtle. The variable pertains to differences among human beings as to their biological rhythm and natural energy level.

Biologists have discovered that every person possesses an inherent biological rhythm, determined genetically and only slightly modifiable within the first two or three years of life, almost never thereafter. Biological rhythm shows up in speech patterns, body movements, emotional responses, and is part of what we often call "temperament." Closely related to the foregoing is the fact that some people are naturally and inherently more energetic than others, physically and/or emotionally and/or intellectually: they move, feel, think faster or slower; they react faster or slower; they seem to experience different relationships to time.

To consider this phenomenon first in its negative impact: It sometimes happens that two people meet and are on the verge of falling in love on the basis of many affinities and complementary differences; yet there is a subtle, often mysteriously continuing friction between them. They cannot explain it. They feel strangely "out of sync" with each other. They often feel irritated and have difficulty accounting for their feelings. In such cases, the barrier to their successful relationship may well be incompatible differences in biological rhythm and inherent energy level.

The person who is naturally faster feels chronically impatient; the person who is naturally slower feels chronically pressured. Often, the faster of the two responds by becoming still faster, and the slower of the two responds by becoming still slower, each trying to force the other to accommodate to his or her natural state, unaware that what is being demanded is more or less impossible. Not understanding this phenomenon, they will commonly invent reasons to explain their quarrels and disagreements; they will look for faults in each other; and when they break apart they will explain the break in terms of these alleged faults. They will remain unaware of the deeper reasons for their incompatibility.

Of course, men and women can and do fall in love sometimes in spite of this area of conflict. And sometimes there are enough other positives in their relationship—and the couple has enough art and wisdom—so that they are able to rise above this difficulty. But sometimes—often—the difficulty proves to be an insurmountable barrier to a sustaining love. And what is sad is how rarely the couple understands why.

To consider the happy side of this phenomenon: When a man and a woman meet and feel "in sync" in this area, there can be an exhilarating experience of harmony, of "rightness" about the relationship (when this basic affinity is supported by other affinities). There is the experience of "knowing" the other in a very special sense. When we see a couple who have other basic affinities and who, in addition, are relatively well synchronized in their biological rhythm and inherent energy level, we often sense a marvelous kind of resonance between them, as if they are moving to the same silent music.

We are far from fully understanding differences among people in this area. It is not easy to provide a principle that will explain why some measure of differences are tolerable and others seem not to be. At the present level of our knowledge, this is a phenomenon that we chiefly know from direct experience, by feeling, by sensing it in ourselves and in others. But once we become aware of it, once we notice it, once we look at our relationships in the context of this understanding, a fresh illumination is often provided. We understand an additional reason why we felt more compellingly attracted to one person than to any other, or why, in a love relationship that almost happened but didn't, or that began and failed, it was possible for us to enjoy so many areas of harmony and compatibility and yet to feel emotionally undercut and undermined by some subtle but inescapably irritating friction.

Love as a Private Universe

Out of the basic affinities and complementary differences that generate romantic love, we create a private world. Two selves, two personalities, two senses of life, two islands of consciousness have found each other, have interpenetrated, have begun to develop the space they will inhabit so long as the relationship lasts. The new universe that is created is not the same as the universe that either person occupied alone: it is the result of an intermingling.

This is the universe we come home to in the evening, when we rejoin our partner. It is a universe made of silent understandings and unspoken words, of eloquent glances and humorous shorthand signals, a universe of shared subjectivity. Everyone who has been in love more than once knows that each love relationship has its own music, its own emotional quality, its own style—and its own world.

And whether it is a universe based on shared sight (romantic love) or one based on shared blindness (immature love), whether it is a universe shaped by happiness or one that is merely a fortress against pain, it is—by its nature—by the nature of love, mature or immature—an emotional support system, a sanctuary, a source of nourishment and energy, apart from the outside world. Sometimes it is experienced as the only point of certainty, the only thing solid and real, in the midst of chaos and ambiguity.

Indeed, this is one of the needs filled by romantic love: *The need for the support provided by that pri-*

vate universe, the fuel it offers for the outside struggles of our existence. If the love relationship is successful at all, such a universe always *begins* as a source of support; whether or not it will remain so depends on the man and woman who create it.

A man and woman meet and fall in love, and the creation of their unique universe begins in the first moment, then keeps evolving as the relationship evolves, as each of them evolves.

Having fallen in love, having committed themselves to each other, having chosen to join forces, they now stand before one of the most formidable of all human undertakings: *to make their relationship work.*

We have considered what love is and why it is born. We shall now consider why it sometimes grows, and why it sometimes dies. We shall examine the challenges of romantic love.

FOUR

•

The Challenges of Romantic Love

Prologue: The Challenges Ahead

The task of defining the conditions necessary and sufficient to fulfill and sustain a romantic-love relationship may appear as difficult as defining those necessary and sufficient for the creation of a great symphony. We can lay down that which seems clearly necessary, but can we be certain that we have identified that which is sufficient as well? And even conditions that seem clearly necessary can at times be broken, or at least bent a little. So the assignment may be viewed as formidable, not because of anything inherently unknowable or mystical, but because of the richness and complexity of human psychology.

Of course, there are many people who are heavily invested in the belief that love is inherently mysterious and mocks all efforts at rational understanding. Such people may even believe that understanding kills romantic love. This is tantamount to saying that consciousness kills.

The exact opposite is true. Unconsciousness kills. Ignorance kills. Blindness kills. If we cannot deepen our grasp of at least some of the essentials needed for the success of romantic love, then there is nothing waiting ahead but more centuries of the same suffering between man and woman that we have behind us.

I do not believe that suffering is the necessary and inevitable condition of human beings here on earth. I do not believe that the essence of life is misery. But I am entirely convinced that that belief is itself a major *cause* of human misery. The teachings of religion to the contrary notwithstanding, resignation to pain is no particular virtue. Quite the contrary. Indeed, here is the problem: people are all too tolerant of suffering, all too quick to tell themselves, in effect, "So who's happy?"

Resignation to uncontested suffering is merely passivity, a failure to take responsibility for one's own existence. It may indeed be the ultimate human vice. Sometimes, when I work with people in psychotherapy or at my Intensives and I see an attitude of sulking, of self-indulgent self-pity, of the avoidance of any responsibility for the solving of problems, it is very difficult not to feel impatient, not to feel that the people involved truly invite their misery. They appear to be waiting—sullenly, resentfully, helplessly, with *assumed* helplessness—for someone else to create their happiness. This cannot be done.

But to take responsibility for our existence, we need to relinquish the belief that frustration and defeat are our natural and inevitable fate. That belief, which is sometimes upheld as an expression of higher sophistication or wisdom, is in fact a default on the very challenge of being alive, of being conscious, of being human.

There are reasons why love grows and there are reasons why love dies. We may not know everything on the subject but we know a great deal.

This said, let us consider the major challenges that must be met successfully if the promise of romantic love is to be realized. In considering these challenges we shall be dealing simultaneously with the questions of why love sometimes grows and why love sometimes dies. It would be artificial to attempt to deal with these questions separately; they are two sides of the same coin. The positive and negative aspects will be used to illuminate each other; they will be interwoven throughout.

Self-Esteem

Of the various factors that are vital for the success of romantic love, none is more important than self-esteem. The first love affair we must consummate successfully is the love affair with ourselves. Only then are we ready for other love relationships.

It has become something of a cliché to observe that, if we do not love ourselves, we cannot love anyone else. This is true enough, but it is only part of the picture. If we do not love ourselves, it is almost impossible to believe fully that we *are loved* by someone else. It is almost impossible to *accept* love. It is almost impossible to *receive* love. No matter what our partner does to show that he or she cares, we do not experience the devotion as convincing because we do not feel lovable to ourselves.

I have written elsewhere of the central and powerful role of self-esteem in our life and experience (Branden, 1969). But a brief review of certain core ideas is needed here to establish an understanding of the relationship between self-esteem and our capacity for fulfillment in love relationships.

Self-esteem, as a psychological phenomenon, has two interrelated aspects: a sense of personal efficacy and a sense of personal worth. It is the integrated sum of self-confidence and self-respect. It is the conviction —or, more precisely, the *experience*—that we are *competent* to live and *worthy* of living. Self-esteem is the experience that we are appropriate to life and to its requirements and challenges.

If an individual felt inadequate to face the challenges of life, if an individual lacked fundamental self-trust, trust in his or her mind, we would recognize the presence of a self-esteem deficiency. And if an individual lacked a basic sense of self-respect, lacked a sense of being worthy, of being entitled to the assertion of legitimate needs and wants, again we would recognize a self-esteem deficiency. Both elements are indispensable to healthy self-esteem: a sense of basic *competence* and a sense of basic *worth*.

To experience that I am competent to live means confidence in the functioning of my mind, in my ability to understand and judge the facts of reality within the sphere of my interests and needs; intellectual self-trust; intellectual self-reliance.

To experience that I am worthy of living means an affirmative attitude toward my right to live and to be happy, toward the assertion of my own wants and needs, the feeling that happiness is my natural birthright.

Self-esteem exists along a continuum: it is not the case that an individual either has self-esteem or lacks it. It is a matter of degree. It is hard to imagine an individual entirely devoid of *any* vestige of self-esteem. It is also hard to envision an individual without any further capacity to grow in self-esteem.

We are not concerned here with all the psychological factors that contribute to a given person's level of self-esteem. We only need recognize the obvious fact that different persons experience different levels of self-esteem, and that the level of our self-esteem has a profound impact on our life and experience.

The nature and level of our self-esteem affects virtually every aspect of our life. It affects our choice of the person we fall in love with and our behavior in the relationship. We have already noted that people with similar self-esteem levels tend to seek each other out. We tend to feel most comfortable, most "at home," with persons whose self-esteem level resembles our own.

High-self-esteem individuals tend to be attracted to other high-self-esteem individuals; medium-self-esteem individuals tend to be attracted to medium-self-esteem individuals; low-self-esteem individuals tend to be attracted to other low-self-esteem individuals. When I speak of being "attracted," I am not talking of a momentary sexual response but of the kind of attachment we are likely to describe as "love."

We cannot understand the tragedy of most relationships if we do not understand that the overwhelming majority of human beings suffer from some feelings of self-esteem deficiency. This means, among other things, that deep in their psyche they do not feel they are "enough": they do not feel lovable as they are; they do not feel it is "natural" or "normal" for others to love them. They do not necessarily hold these attitudes consciously. On the conscious level they may say, "Of course I expect to be loved. Of course I deserve to be loved. Why shouldn't I be?" But the deeper, negative feelings are there, operating to sabotage efforts at achieving fulfillment.

In classes on literature we are taught that "character determines action." I would paraphrase that to say self-concept determines destiny. Or, to speak with greater restraint and precision, there is a strong *tendency* for self-concept to determine destiny.

If, for example, we have trust in ourselves, trust in our ability to understand, trust in the competence of our mind, we will be open to experience, motivated to understand, motivated to exert the effort to understand. We will not be frozen or paralyzed by the blocks generated by self-doubt. And our growing competence will enhance our feelings of self-trust.

If, on the other hand, we experience a deep doubt of our efficacy, if we lack confidence in our cognitive ability, if we distrust our judgment, our very insecurities will lead to behaviors that result in frustration and defeat. These behaviors, and the results they lead to, seem to justify our initial self-distrust.

Here is another example of how such self-fulfilling prophecies operate. I recall an incident when I was lecturing to a college audience on the psychology of romantic love. Afterward, a group of students crowded around with questions. Among them was a young woman who began by complimenting me on my talk and then went on to say, quite bitterly, how much she wished "men" would understand the principles I had been discussing. As she went on talking, I became aware of an impulse to withdraw from her, to turn away. At the same time, I was intrigued by my reaction because I was in a very good mood that evening and feeling very benevolently disposed toward the whole world. She was delivering a monologue to the effect that men did not appreciate intelligence in women and I stopped her by saying, "Listen, I'd like to share something with you. Right now I'm feeling an impulse to break off talking with you. I am feeling an impulse to avoid you. And I think I know how it's happening. I would like to tell you about it, if you're interested." Taken aback, she nodded, and I went on, "As you began to talk, I received three messages from you. First, I received the impression that you liked me and wanted me to like you, wanted me to respond to you positively. Second, and at the same time, I got the message that you were already convinced I could not possibly like you or be interested in anything you had to say. Third, and again at the same time, I got the message that you were angry at me for rejecting you. And I had not yet opened my mouth to say a word to you." She became thoughtful, and then smiled sadly in recognition, and acknowledged the truth of my description. I said, "What's fortunate for you right now is that I'm willing to explain myself. But if you're talking to some young man, and sending out these messages, very likely he's just going to walk away. And, watching his disappearing back, you're going to tell yourself the problem is that men don't appreciate intelligent women. And you're going to be blind to your own role in creating the very situation over which you are suffering."

It is evident that self-concept tends to determine destiny in romantic love. Let us now consider more specifically how.

The Appropriateness of Being Loved

Imagine that an individual feels, perhaps beneath the level of conscious awareness, that he or she significantly lacks worth, is not lovable, is not a person who can inspire devotion for any sustained length of time. Simultaneously, this individual desires love, pursues love, hopes and dreams to find love. Let us suppose this person is a man. He finds a woman he cares for, she seems to care for him, they are happy, excited, and stimulated in each other's presence—and for a time it seems that his dream is to be fulfilled. But deep in his psyche a time bomb is ticking away—the belief that he is inherently unlovable.

This time bomb provokes him to destroy his relationship. He may do this in any number of ways. He may endlessly demand reassurance. He may become excessively possessive and jealous. He may behave cruelly to "test" the depth of her devotion to him. He may make self-deprecating comments and wait for her to correct him. He may tell her he does not deserve her and tell her again and again and again. He may tell her that no woman can be trusted and that all women are fickle. He may find endless excuses to criticize her, to reject her before she can reject him. He may attempt to control and manipulate her by making her feel guilty, thereby hoping to bind her to him. He may become silent, withdrawn, preoccupied, throwing up barriers she cannot penetrate.

After a while, perhaps, she has had enough; she is exhausted; he has worn her out. She leaves him.

He feels desolate, depressed, crushed, devastated. It is wonderful. He has been proven right. The world is the way he always knew it was. "They're writing songs of love, but not for me." But how satisfying it is to know that one understands the nature of reality!

Suppose that, despite his best efforts, he cannot

drive her away. Perhaps she believes in him, sees his potential. Or perhaps she has a masochistic streak that requires that she be involved with such a man. She clings to him; she keeps reassuring him. Her devotion grows stronger, no matter what he does. She simply does not understand the nature of the universe as he perceives it. She does not grasp that no one can love him. In continuing to love him, she presents him with a problem: She confounds his view of reality. He needs a solution. He needs a way out.

He finds it. He decides that he has fallen out of love with her. Or he tells himself that she bores him. Or he tells himself that he is now in love with someone else. Or he tells himself that love does not interest him. The particular choice does not matter; the net effect is the same: in the end, he is alone again—the way he always "knew" he would be.

Then, once more, he can dream of finding love—he can look for a new woman—so that he can play out the drama all over again.

It is not essential, of course, that his relationship end so conclusively. A literal separation may not be necessary. He may be willing to allow a relationship to continue, providing both he and his partner are unhappy. This is a compromise he can live with. It is as good as being alone and abandoned—almost.

Suppose, to give another example, that a woman decides a man could not possibly prefer her to other women. Her self-concept cannot accommodate such a possibility. At the same time, being human, she longs for love. When she finds it, what does she typically proceed to do?

She may continually compare herself unfavorably to other women. She may go out of her way to make absurd pretentions at superiority, denying and disowning her feelings of insecurity. She may keep pointing out attractive women to see how he will respond. She may torment him with her doubts and suspicions. She may even encourage him to have affairs, suggesting that it might be good for him and she wouldn't mind. One way or the other, she creates a situation that results in her lover's becoming involved with someone else.

Of course she suffers acutely. She is desolate. But her situation is gratifying beyond words. She has created the very state of affairs she always "knew" would come about.

Now let us observe, as an aside, that the desire to be in control of our lives is entirely human; it is hardly irrational. But it can lead to irrational behavior, when we are unconsciously manipulated by our self-destructive and self-sabotaging beliefs. To be "in control" means to understand the facts of reality that bear on our life so that we are able to predict, with reasonable accuracy, the consequences of our actions. Tragedy occurs when, out of a *misguided* notion of control, we attempt to "adjust" reality to our beliefs, rather than to adjust our beliefs to reality. Tragedy occurs when we cling to our beliefs blindly and manipulate events without awareness of doing so, insensitive to the fact that alternative possibilities exist. Tragedy occurs when we would rather be "right" than happy, when we would rather sustain the *illusion* that we are "in control" than notice that reality is not the way we have told ourselves it is.

If we hold negative self-concepts of which we are unaware, if we hold self-sabotaging beliefs of which we are unconscious, we are their prisoner. Only when we become conscious of our self-sabotaging beliefs do we become able to change our behavior.

As we see ourselves, so do we act. And our actions tend to produce results that continually support our self-concept.

With a *positive* self-concept, this principle can work in our favor. With a *negative* self-concept, it results in disaster.

When we feel rejected, when we look at past relationships and see nothing but a string of disappointments, frustrations, and defeats, it is often illuminating to ask: Do I feel it is natural or normal for someone to love me? Or does it feel like an impossible miracle that could not happen? Or could not last?

The first requirement of happiness in romantic love is a vision of ourselves that contains the *rightness* of being loved, the *naturalness* of being loved, the *appropriateness* of being loved. People who know how to make themselves happy in love relationships are people who are open to *accepting* love. And in order to accept love, they must love themselves. People who love themselves do not find it incomprehensible that others should love them. They are able to *allow* others to love them. Their love has ease and grace.

As we proceed we shall see more and more clearly how essential an accomplished self-esteem is in this aspect of life. *To enjoy our own being, to be happy in a profound sense with who we are, to experience the self as worthy of being valued and loved by others—this is the first requirement for the growth of romantic love.*

The Appropriateness of Being Happy

Contained in the experience of self-esteem, as I have already indicated, is the sense of our right to assert our own interests, needs, and wants: the experience of feeling worthy of happiness.

Working with thousands of people in a variety of professional contexts and settings, I have been struck again and again by the prevalence of people's fear and doubt in this area, their feeling that they do not deserve happiness, that they are not entitled to the fulfillment of their wants. Often there is the feeling that if they are happy either happiness will be taken away from them or something terrible will happen to counter-balance it, some unspeakable punishment or tragedy. Happiness, for such people, is a potential source of anxiety. While they may long for it on one level of consciousness, they dread it on another.

A person may insist, "Of course I'm entitled to happiness!" On the conscious level there may be a normal longing for it, including the felicity associated with romantic love. But when happiness is actually experienced, when the person is in a relationship that is working, often the response is a feeling of anxiety and disorientation. There is the wordless sense of "This is not the way my life is supposed to be."

Many an individual, particularly if raised in a religious home, has been taught that suffering represents a passport to salvation, whereas enjoyment is almost certainly proof that one has strayed from the proper path. Psychotherapy clients have spoken to me of times when, as children, they were ill, and a parent told them, "Don't regret that you are in pain. Every day you suffer, you are piling up credits in heaven." What is the implication? What is one piling up on the days when one is happy?

Or the child has been encouraged to feel, "Don't be so excited. Happiness doesn't last. When you grow up, you'll realize how grim life is."

For such people, to experience themselves as happy may be to experience themselves as, in effect, out of step with reality—therefore in danger. When will the lightning bolt strike?

Now suppose that a man and woman who share this orientation meet and fall in love. In the beginning, focused on each other and on the excitement of their relationship, they are not thinking of these matters; they are simply happy. But inside, the time bomb is ticking. It began ticking at the moment of their first meeting.

Facing one another across a dinner table, feeling joyful and contented, one of them suddenly can't stand it and starts a quarrel over nothing or withdraws and becomes mysteriously depressed.

They cannot allow the happiness just to be there; they cannot leave it alone; they cannot simply enjoy the fact that they have found each other. Their sense of who they are, and of what their proper destiny is, cannot accommodate happiness. The impulse to make trouble arises, seemingly from nowhere, actually from the deep recesses of the psyche where the antihappiness "programming" resides.

Their view of self, and of the universe, allows them, perhaps, to *struggle* for happiness—to yearn for happiness—"sometime in the future"—perhaps next year—or the year after that. But not now. Not at this moment. Not here. Here and now is too terrifyingly close, too terrifyingly immediate.

Right now, in the moment of their joy, happiness is not a dream but a reality. That is unbearable. First of all, they don't deserve it. Second, it can't last. Third, if it does last, something else terrible will happen. This is one of the commonest responses of people who suffer from a significant lack of self-esteem, of confidence in their right to be happy.

I am continually impressed by the fact that whenever I raise this issue in my Intensives on *Self-Esteem and the Art of Being* or *Self-Esteem and Romantic Relationships,* the majority of those present respond to the point immediately; very little explanation seems needed; they are very familiar with the phenomenon. Some are defensive, some struggle to avoid coming to grips with the problem, but the majority—interestingly enough—respond honestly, if sadly. Once the issue is pointed out, they notice readily how often they interrupt their own happiness, sabotage it, create trouble where none need exist—do anything to escape the fact that they can be happy *right now,* if only they will accept the moment, not fight it, not resist, just yield to the joy of being, yield to the joy of each other, yield to the ecstatic potential of romantic love. But no, they prefer to take workshops, consult marriage counselors, enter psychotherapy, study sex manuals, accumulate books on psychology, so that they can make themselves happy *in the future,* at some unspecified time, a time that never comes, like the horizon that keeps receding as one approaches.

Sometimes I will ask a group, "How many of you have had the experience of waking up one morning and noticing that in spite of all sorts of problems, difficulties, worries, you feel wonderful, you feel happy, you feel delighted to be alive? And after a while, you can't stand it, you have to do something. So you manage to fling yourself back into a state of misery. Or perhaps you are with someone you really care about and you're feeling very contented, very fulfilled, and then feelings of anxiety or disorientation arise and you feel the impulse to stir up conflict, to make trouble. You can't keep out of the way and allow happiness to happen. You feel the need to throw a little 'drama' into your life." Inevitably, at least half the hands in the room go up.

The evidence is clear: for a great many people, *happiness-anxiety* is a very real problem—and a powerful barrier to romantic love.

Happiness-anxiety is itself not an uncommon consequence of the failure to achieve adequate separation and individuation. Poor self-esteem and inadequate separation and individuation go hand in hand; they are intimately linked. Without successful separation and individuation, I do not sufficiently discover my own internal resources; I do not discover my own strength; I can very easily persist in the belief that my survival depends on protecting my relationship with my mother and father, at the expense of enjoying the rest of my life. Let us consider where this can lead.

Suppose that a woman has witnessed the unhappy marriage of her parents. It is not uncommon for a child to internalize a subtle message from Mother or Father to the effect, "You are not to be any happier in your marriage than I was in mine." A woman with inadequate self-esteem, a woman who wants to be a "good girl," who feels the need to retain Mother's or Father's love at all costs, often proceeds very obediently either to select a husband with whom happiness is clearly impossible or to manufacture unhappiness in a marriage where happiness might have been possible. Many women have reported the feeling, "I couldn't bear to let Mother see that I was happy in my relationship with a man. She would feel betrayed, she would feel humiliated. I might cause her to feel overwhelmed by her own sense of inadequacy and failure. And I couldn't do that to her." But beneath these statements are other, clearly evident, feelings. "Mother might become angry at me, Mother might repudiate me, I might lose Mother's love" (Friday, 1977).

To be unhappy, as Mother or Father were, is to "belong." To be happy may mean to stand alone, against Mother or Father, perhaps against the whole family—and that prospect may be terrifying.

The problem may exist between a woman and her mother or between a woman and her father. And the problem is not confined to women. Men, too, can receive messages from either parent to the effect that they are not to be happy romantically. For many persons, to be happy romantically means no longer to be a "good girl" or a "good boy." To be happy romantically may mean to separate from one's family. This demands a level of independence that many women and men do not achieve. Here we observe the interpenetration of the themes of separation and individuation, self-esteem deficiency, and happiness-anxiety.

If we feel that our relationships always seem to be unhappy, always seem to be frustrating, it is relevant to inquire: Am I allowed to be happy? Does my self-concept permit it? Does my view of the universe permit it? Does my childhood programming permit it? Does my life scenario permit it?

If the answer is in the negative, it is futile to try to solve romantic problems by learning communications skills, improved sexual techniques, or methods of "fair fighting." This is what is wrong with so much marriage counseling. All such teachings rest on the assumption that the persons involved are *willing* to be happy, *want* to be happy, feel *entitled* to be happy. But what if they don't.

The growth of love in romantic relationships requires an appreciation of the fact that happiness is our human birthright.

If happiness feels natural to me, feels normal, I can allow it, can be open to it, can flow with it; I do not feel the impulse to sabotage and self-destruct.

When there is an accepting attitude toward happiness, romantic love grows. When there is a fearful attitude toward happiness, romantic love tends to die.

For some individuals, the simple act of allowing themselves to be happy, with the independence and self-responsibility that implies, may be the most heroic act life will ever require of them.

How are they to proceed? What are they to do if happiness triggers anxiety? The desire to reduce anxiety is obviously normal. And if happiness ignites anxiety, then the impulse to reduce or sabotage happiness is very understandable. It is a thoroughly human response.

A better solution exists, but it must be discovered, it must be learned—and then it must be practiced.

When we feel happy, and that happiness triggers anxiety and disorientation, we must learn to do *nothing* —that is, to breathe into our feelings, to allow them, to watch our own process, to enter into the depths of our own experience while at the same time being a conscious witness to it *and not be manipulated into behaving self-destructively*. Then, across time, we can build a tolerance for happiness, we can increase our ability to handle joy without panicking.

Slowly, in this manner, we discover that a new way of being is possible. We discover that being happy is far less complicated than we had believed. We discover that, given half a chance, joy is our natural state.

Then . . . romantic love is allowed to grow.

Autonomy

Romantic love is for grown-ups; it is not for children. It is not for children in a literal sense, and also in a psychological sense: not for those who, regardless of age, still experience themselves as children.

Let us remind ourselves of the meaning of autonomy.

Autonomy pertains to an individual's capacity for self-direction and self-regulation. Autonomy and self-esteem are inseparable; both presuppose successful separation and individuation.

Autonomous individuals understand that other people do not exist merely to satisfy their needs. They have accepted the fact that no matter how much love and caring may exist between persons, we are each of us, in an ultimate sense, responsible for ourselves.

Autonomous individuals have grown beyond the need to prove to anyone that they are a good boy or a good girl, just as they have outgrown the need for their spouse or romantic partner also to be their mother or father. This does not nullify the fact that they may experience moments when they would like their partner to function in that role; that can be quite normal, but it does not form the essence of their relationships.

They are ready for romantic love because they have grown up, because they do not experience themselves as waifs waiting to be rescued or saved; they do not require anyone else's permission to be who they are, and their egos are not continually "on the line."

This last issue is important and needs elaboration. An autonomous individual is one who does not experience his or her self-esteem as continually in question or in jeopardy. His or her worth is not a matter of continuing doubt. The source of approval resides within the self. It is not at the mercy of every encounter with another person.

In the best of relationships there are occasional frictions, unavoidable hurts, times when individuals "miss" one another in their responses. The tendency of nonautonomous, immature individuals is to translate such incidents into evidence of rejection, evidence of not really being loved, so small frictions or failures of communication are easily escalated into major conflicts.

Autonomous individuals have a greater capacity to "roll with the punches," to see the normal frictions of everyday life in realistic perspective, not to get their feelings hurt over trivia, or, even if they are hurt occasionally, not to catastrophize such moments.

Further, autonomous individuals respect their partner's need to follow his or her own destiny, to be alone sometimes, to be preoccupied sometimes, *not* to be thinking about the relationship sometimes, but rather about other vital matters that may not even involve the partner in any direct sense, such as work, personal unfolding and evolution, personal developmental needs. So autonomous individuals do not always need to be "center stage," do not need always to be the focus of attention, do not panic when the partner is mentally preoccupied elsewhere. Autonomous individuals give this freedom to themselves as well as to those they love.

This is the reason why, between autonomous men and women, romantic love can grow. And this is the reason why, between nonautonomous men and women, romantic love so often dies: panicky clinging suffocates love.

No matter how passionate the commitment and devotion autonomous men and women may feel toward the one they love, there is still the recognition that space must exist, freedom must exist, sometimes aloneness must exist. There is the recognition that no matter how intensely we love, we are none of us "only" lovers —we are also, in a broader sense, evolving human beings.

Autonomous individuals have assimilated and integrated the ultimate fact of human aloneness. Not resisting it, not denying it, they do not experience it as a burning pain or a tragedy in their lives. Therefore, they are not constantly engaged in the effort to achieve, through their relationships, the illusion that such aloneness does not exist. They understand that it is the fact of aloneness that gives romantic love its unique intensity. Their harmony with aloneness is what makes them uniquely competent to participate in romantic love.

When two self-responsible human beings find each other, when they fall in love, they are able, to a degree far above the average, to appreciate each other, to enjoy each other, to see each other for what he or she is, precisely because the other is not viewed as the means of avoiding the fact that each must be responsible for him- or herself.

Then they can fall into each other's arms, then they can love each other, then sometimes one can play the child and the other the parent—and it doesn't matter, because it is only a game, it is only a moment's rest; each knows the ultimate truth and is not afraid of it, has made peace with it, has understood the essence of our humanity.

When we have not matured to the point of being able to accept the fact of our ultimate aloneness, when we are frightened of it, when we try to deny it, we tend to overburden our relationships with an unhealthy dependence that stifles and suffocates them. We do not embrace, we cling. Without air and open spaces, love cannot breathe.

This is the paradox: *only when we stop fighting the fact of our aloneness are we ready for romantic love.*

Realistic Romanticism

Perhaps one of the clearest requirements for a successful romantic relationship is that it be based on a foundation of realism. This is the ability and willingness to see our partner as he or she is, with shortcomings as well as virtues, rather than attempting to carry on a romance with a fantasy.

To deal first with the negative case: If I do not see and love my partner as a real person in the real world, if instead I elaborate a fantasy about him or her, using the person merely as a springboard for my imagination and my wishes, then I am doomed sooner or later to resent the actual person for not living up to my fantasies. If I choose to pretend that my partner does not have the shortcomings he or she has, if I refuse to include the knowledge of those shortcomings in the overall picture of my partner, later I am likely not only to feel hurt, outraged, and betrayed but also to cast myself in the role of a bewildered victim. "How can you do this to me?"

The truth is, of course, that on a deeper level, as we have already seen, *we know whom we choose*—but it is easy enough to deny and disown this knowledge when it seems desirable to do so. And if our life scenario dictates that we be a betrayed victim, such self-deception will indeed feel desirable.

One reason why so many men and women seem to fall in love with a fantasy rather than with the actual person they profess to love is that they have a great many disowned needs, disowned longings, disowned hurts, disowned desires which they are consciously unaware of, perhaps, while subconsciously seeking to satisfy, resolve, or heal. A person unaware of his or her own deepest needs can respond to another on the basis of fairly superficial characteristics if some of those characteristics trigger the hope or belief that in the present relationship those needs can be fulfilled. For example, a sensitive, intelligent man who was not popular with girls during his teenage years—perhaps he was too serious or too shy—may in his twenties meet a beautiful young woman who is in type and manner just the kind of girl that he never could have had in adolescence. He is fascinated, he is enchanted, and subconsciously he entertains the hope and expectation that if he can win her it would somehow heal all the hurt and the loneliness of his adolescence; it would wipe away all the past rejections; it would fulfill all the unrealized dreams of those painful, lonely years. None of this is verbalized, of course, none of it is conceptualized, but such are the considerations operating within him. It is easy enough, especially since he is motivated to deceive himself, for him to overlook the fact that he and this woman have nothing in common, neither values nor interests nor sense of life nor outlook on important matters, and that if he were somehow to win her, it would not be very long before she would bore him to death. If she does respond to him, if a relationship forms, there may be a great deal of passion and intensity in the beginning; but there is very little mystery as to why such "love" will die.

On the other hand, when and if we choose to see our partner realistically, not deceiving ourselves, love, if it is real in the first place, has the best of all opportunities to grow. We know whom we are choosing and we are not shocked when our partner acts in character. A very happily married woman once said to me, "An hour after I met the man I married I could have given you a lecture on ways he would be difficult to live with. I think he's the most exciting man I've ever known, but I've never kidded myself about the fact that he's also one of the most self-absorbed. Often he's like an absent minded professor. He spends a great deal of time in a private world of his own. I had to know that going in, or else I would have been very upset later. He never made any pretenses about the kind of man he was. I can't understand people who profess to be hurt or shocked at the way their mates turn out. It's so obvious what people are if you'll just pay attention. I've never been happier in my whole life than I am right now in this marriage. But not because I tell myself my husband is 'perfect' or without fault." She added, "You know, I think that's why I feel so appreciative of his strength and virtues. I'm willing to see everything."

This is realistic romanticism, not fairy-tale romanticism. When passion and sight are integrated, love can flourish.

Mutual Self-Disclosure: The Meaning of Sharing a Life

One of the characteristics of love relationships that flower is a relatively high degree of mutual self-disclosure—a willingness to let our partner enter into the interior of our private world and a genuine interest in the private world of that partner. Couples in love tend to show more of themselves to each other than to any other person.

This implies that they have created an atmosphere of trust and acceptance, but it implies more than that. It implies first and foremost, that each is willing to know and encounter him- or herself. This is the necessary precondition of the willingness for mutual self-disclosure.

And here we confront one of the greatest obstacles to the sustaining of romantic love: the widespread problem of human self-alienation. Self-alienation tends to make self-disclosure impossible.

The problem is not new, but perhaps at no time in history has there been such awareness on the part of so many people of the fact that they suffer from a sense of personal unreality, that they have lost touch with themselves, that too often they do not know what they feel, but they act with numb obliviousness to that which prompts or motivates their actions. For romantic love, the results are disastrous.

The source of this self-alienation—or, as it might better be described, *this unconsciousness*—springs from several factors. To begin with the simplest and most obvious: Many parents *teach* children to repress their feelings. They teach unconsciousness as a positive value, as one of the costs of being loved, found acceptable, regarded as "grown-up." A little boy falls and hurts himself and is told sternly by his father, "Men don't cry." A little girl expresses anger at her brother, or perhaps shows dislike toward an older relative, and is told by the mother, "It's terrible to feel that way. You don't really feel it." A child bursts into the house, full of joy and excitement, and is told by an irritated parent, "What's wrong with you? Why do you make so much noise?"

Children also learn to repress their feelings by example. Emotionally remote and inhibited parents tend to produce emotionally remote and inhibited children, not only through their overt communications but also by their own behavior, which proclaims to the child what is "proper," "appropriate," "socially acceptable."

Parents who accept certain teachings of religion are

very likely to infect their children with the disastrous notion that there are such things as "evil thoughts" or "evil emotions." The child is then filled with moral terror of his or her inner life.

Thus a child can be led to the conclusion that his feelings are potentially dangerous, that sometimes it is advisable to deny them, that they must be "controlled." What such "control" means practically is that a child learns to *disown* his or her own feelings, effectively ceasing to experience them. Needless to say, this process does not take place through conscious, calculated decisions; to a large extent it may be described as subconscious. But the process of self-alienation has begun. In denying feelings, in nullifying his or her judgments and evaluations, in repudiating his or her experience, the child has learned to disown parts of the self, of the personality.

The child begins in a natural state, in contact with his or her organism. And a conflict is set up: the child is taught that certain feelings or emotions are unacceptable. But they are felt. The child produces a solution: *unconsciousness*.

This same strategy is utilized by the child to defend against any feelings which are experienced as threatening or overwhelming: pain, fear, anger, and so forth. It is not only negative feelings that become blocked. Joy, excitement, sexuality can equally become targets of emotional repression—when and if they are experienced by the child as threatening to his or her equilibrium, safety, or self-esteem.

This problem, which originates in childhood, becomes built into the personality, built into an individual's manner of being and of coping with life, so that, by the time he or she is an adult, a condition of self-alienation feels "normal."

Yet that which is disowned and repressed does not cease to exist. On another level, it continues to operate within us. Only it is not integrated. So, to the extent that we suffer from self-disowning, we are in a chronic state of disharmony with ourselves.

Yet in romantic love it is precisely the self that we wish to make visible and to share.

In my Intensive on *Self-Esteem and the Art of Being,* one of our central tasks is the rediscovery and reclaiming of various disowned parts of the self, so that self-esteem can expand and the capacity for love can flower. Sometimes—often, in fact—when submerged parts of the self begin to rise to awareness, there is resistance, there is struggle, there is anxiety and disorientation. "How will people react? Will people still love me if they learn about my anger? Will people still care for me if they learn that I am not so helpless? Will I be abandoned and left alone if I allow my full intelligence to flower and to be seen? Will I still be able to tolerate my job—or my marriage—if I own who I really am, if I own what I really feel and what I really am capable of?"

The point is not that we must act on or express everything we feel, not even in our most intimate relationships. Obviously, in matters of behavior, judgment and discrimination are always needed. Sometimes it may be appropriate to communicate our feelings, sometimes not. Sometimes it may be appropriate to share our thoughts and perceptions, sometimes not. We will say more about that when we turn to the process of communication. Here what needs to be recognized is that *the primary issue is not between us and other people. It is between us and ourselves.*

If we are free to know honestly what we feel and to experience it (not merely to acknowledge it verbally), then we can decide with whom and in what context it is appropriate to share our inner life. But if we ourselves do not know, if we are forbidden to know, if we are afraid to know, if we ourselves have never encountered who we are—if we are self-alienated—then we are crippled and incapacitated for genuine intimacy, which means that we are crippled and incapacitated for romantic love.

So much of the joy of love—so much that nurtures love—has to do with showing and sharing who we are.

Self-disclosure enhances the experience of visibility, makes possible support and validation, stimulates growth. Mutual self-disclosure opens the door to many of the most precious values that we seek in romantic love.

We cannot demand of our lover that he or she applaud everything we feel, think, fantasize, or desire. We "merely" need to be able to express ourselves without fear of moral condemnation or attack, in an atmosphere of respect and acceptance. And we are also bound to create the same atmosphere for our partner. But it is very difficult to give to another person that which we have not learned to give to ourselves. If we have learned to lecture and reproach ourselves for "inappropriate" feelings, emotions, and reactions, we almost certainly will treat others the same way. We will lecture and reproach our partner, we will lecture and reproach our children. We will encourage the person we love to practice the same self-disowning, the same self-alienation that we practice. This is one of the ways we kill love. This is one of the ways we kill passion.

So we must ask ourselves: Do I create a context in which my partner can feel free to share feelings, emotions, thoughts, fantasies, without the fear that I will condemn, attack, launch into a lecture, or simply withdraw? And does my partner create such a context for me?

If we cannot answer these questions in the affirmative, we need not wonder at the failure of our relationship. If we *can* answer in the affirmative, we understand a great deal about its success. When a man and woman feel free to share their fantasies, to express their wants, acknowledge their feelings, and communicate concerning their thoughts, with each confident of the other's interest and engagement in the process, then they are masters of one of the most essential elements in fulfilled romantic love.

Communicating Emotions

Romantic-love relationships are made or broken by the effectiveness or ineffectiveness of communication. The essence of mutual self-disclosure is communication. And no element of communication is more important to romantic love than that of feelings and emotions.

Pain

Sometimes we feel hurt, we are in pain. We experience a desire to express our state to the person we love. We experience a need to talk about it, to express whatever is happening within us.

What we want from our partner is interest, the desire and willingness to listen. We want our emotions to be taken seriously, to be respected. We do not wish to be told, "You shouldn't feel that." Or "It's foolish to feel that." We do not wish to be lectured. Very often the healing is achieved, or the solution is found, through the simple act of expressing our pain. Nothing more is needed. We want our partner to understand that. And our partner needs the same understanding from us. When each can give this understanding to the other, the bond of love is strengthened.

But sometimes it is very hard for one partner to give the other what that person would like because the partner does not allow the self freedom to experience and accept his or her own suffering. So how can one person give to another what that person cannot give the self?

In fact, by talking about pain, by seeking to express it, a man or woman may activate disowned and denied pain in the partner, which will first appear, very often, in the form of anxiety. Out of the wish to escape anxiety, the person cuts the speaker off. The partner does not intend to be cruel, does not really understand what is happening. But communication has failed, and the other may feel abandoned.

The greatest gift we can sometimes give a person we love is just to listen, just to be there, just to be available, without any obligation to say something brilliant, or to find a solution, or to cheer our partner up. But to be able to give that to another, we must be able to give it to ourselves. If we are harsh and moralistically judgmental toward our self, we will not treat our partner any better. Self-acceptance is the foundation of acceptance of others. The acceptance of our own feelings is the foundation of our acceptance of the feelings of others.

This is an art that can be practiced, an art that can be learned, by a simple decision to begin, based on an understanding of the principles we are discussing.

But suppose that it is we ourselves who have somehow contributed to the pain our partner is experiencing? Nothing changes; the principle is the same. The appropriate response is to listen, to give our partner the experience of being heard, to show that we care, to acknowledge our error honestly if we have made one, and to take whatever corrective action seems appropriate. But first—to listen, to accept—not necessarily to agree with, but to accept our partner's feelings for what they are, and in any event, not to turn into a punitive parent.

Fear

Sometimes we experience fear, or our partner experiences fear. It helps to be able to express this fear, to talk about it, but often this is very difficult. Most of us have been taught that fear is an emotion to be hidden, to be concealed. We associate being afraid with humiliation. We associate it with "loss of face." We associate "strength" with *lying,* with pretending that we do not feel what we feel.

If we can express our fear with honesty and dignity, or listen to our partner's expression of fear with respect and acceptance, something beautiful can happen. Two people can draw closer. The fear itself, through being accepted and expressed, through being discharged, can disappear. Or, at minimum, we can gather the courage to act against the fear—for example, to submit to surgery that is medically necessary, or to undertake some difficult task in our career, or simply to face and be honest about some difficult truth.

But here again, we deal with the problem of self-acceptance: How much better can we respond to the fear in our partner than we respond to the fear in ourself? Can we give our partner permission to feel that which we cannot give ourself permission to feel? Kindness always begins at home—with kindness to the self.

If communication is to be successful, if love is to be successful, if relationships are to be successful, we must give up the absurd notion that there is something "heroic" or "strong" about lying, about faking what we feel, about misrepresenting, by commission or omission, the reality of our experience or the truth of our being. We must learn that if heroism and strength mean anything, it is the willingness to face reality, to face truth, to respect facts, to accept that that which is, is.*

Anger

Sometimes we are angry with our partner, or our partner is angry with us. This is entirely normal: it is part of life, it does not mean that love has gone.

To express anger honestly, to express feelings honestly—to describe what we see, or what we have observed, or what we think has happened—and to describe how we feel about it—clears the air, opens the door to productive communication.

This is entirely different from attacking our partner's character, "psychologizing" about our partner's motives: "You are always irresponsible!" "You did this only to hurt me!" "You are just like my last husband (wife)!" Such expressions are intended not to communicate but to cause pain, and, generally speaking, they succeed. They succeed in causing pain—and in inspiring counterattack—but they do *not* succeed in achieving productive communication or conflict resolution.

There is an art to expressing anger, and it is an art

---

*As I discuss in *The Disowned Self,* when we deny and repress unwanted feelings, we remain stuck in them, imprisoned; when we allow ourselves to experience them fully, we discharge them and begin to move beyond them. Change becomes possible, growth becomes possible.

imperative for lovers to learn. The art does not consist of denying or disowning anger. The art does not consist of smiling while inwardly burning. The art consists of being honest. Honest about what? *About one's own feelings.* (Ginott, 1972)

If we wish to be in a love relationship, we owe to our partner the freedom for him or her to express anger. We owe it to our partner to listen, not to interrupt, not to fight back, but to listen. After our partner is finished, after he or she feels satisfied about having said everything, then and then only is it appropriate to respond. Then, if we believe our partner has misinterpreted the facts, we can point that out. If it is clear that we are in the wrong, the solution is to acknowledge that.

Relationships are not destroyed by honest expressions of anger. But relationships die every day as a consequence of anger that is not expressed. The repression of anger kills love, kills sex, kills passion.

In order to repress anger, we often "turn off" to the person who has inspired the anger. We "solve" the problem of our anger by making ourselves numb. Relationships are buried by such "solutions."

It is to our self-interest to know that if our partner is angry at us, he or she will tell us so. It is *not* to our self-interest to have one who never complains about things that hurt or anger him or her.

The willingness to share our pain, our fear, and our anger serves the growth of romantic love. Unwillingness to do so subverts its growth.

So we must ask ourselves: To what extent do I create a context in which my partner feels comfortable sharing such feelings with me? To what extent do I feel comfortable sharing such feelings with him or her?

Love, Joy, Excitement

Communication is the lifeblood of a relationship, and this includes, of course, not merely the communication of unhappy feelings, such as those we have just discussed, but also the communication of love, of joy, of excitement, not only the communication of emotions, but also the communication of perceptions, thoughts, fantasies—in other words, the full range of our mental and emotional world.

To "share a life" means far more than merely to live in the same house or to "keep company" with someone; it means to share our inner processes, our inner experience, all that pertains to the self.

This observation seems so obvious, and yet, working with people, it is impossible to escape the conclusion that it is one of the least understood facts of our existence.

Expressing feelings of love and appreciation and desire is vital to the sustaining of a passionate relationship. And yet very often we observe that people are afraid to express such feelings, afraid to put their feelings into words, afraid to show how much they care, how deeply they feel, so they invent transparently absurd rationalizations to explain their lack of such communications. "I married you, didn't I? What more is necessary? Doesn't that show I love you?"

And stranger still, perhaps, there is often fear of being the *recipient* of expressions of love or appreciation or desire. Often the person feels uncomfortable. Perhaps he or she feels undeserving. Perhaps he or she feels an obligation to say or do something clever or inspired, when all that is required is to listen, to accept, to be there.

But what should we do if we experience fear of such intimacy? The solution, as always, is to accept our feelings, to own the fear, to admit it honestly, to allow it to be experienced and expressed, so that it then becomes possible to move beyond it, not to be forever imprisoned by it.

We need to ask ourselves: Can I accept my partner's expressions of love? Of joy? Of excitement? Can I allow my partner to feel, to experience, and to convey such states, whether or not I am always fully able to share them? Or do I turn my partner off, as others once turned me off, as, perhaps, I have learned to turn myself off?

Small wonder that people who cannot handle the realm of emotion—either happy emotions or unhappy ones—complain that inevitably "passion dies." The miracle, perhaps, is not that for them passion dies but that passion ever existed at all, even for a moment. That it can and does is a tribute to the power of the life force within us, which, breaking through the barrier of our repression and self-alienation, however briefly, points the way to the possibility of ecstasy. Our task is to learn not to betray that possibility.

We shall have more to say, later in the chapter, about our fear of excitement, in ourself and in others. But let us consider next the issue of communicating our wants.

Wants

If I am afraid to know what I want or to express it unambiguously, then too often, rather than own the fear, I blame my partner; I feel hurt and resentment over the fact that my partner has failed to provide that which I have not taken responsibility for knowing I want, let alone communicating it.

Often there is a great fear of knowing what we want and a greater fear still of expressing to our partner what we want. There is fear that our partner will not care, will not respond. There is fear that we will put ourselves in his or her hands, give the partner too much "power"—through letting the partner see our naked feelings and desires. There is fear of self-assertion and there is fear of surrendering to love. There is fear of self-expression.

Instead of communication, there is silence, and hurt, and resentment, and self-created loneliness.

We can readily understand how such a situation arises, we can readily understand why it is so common, when we realize how rare it is for a child to be taught that his or her wants matter, how rare it is for a child, even a child who is loved, to have the experience of being taken *seriously* as a human being, to have his or her feelings taken seriously.

If we wish to succeed at romantic love, we need to be aware of the questions: Do I know what I want? Am I willing to express what I want? And do I accept the fact that another person may not always be able to give me what I want—or may not choose to give me what I want? Can I allow for that?

Sometimes people justify not asking their partner for what they want by saying, "Suppose I ask and nothing happens? Suppose there is no response?" The answer is: Ask again. And if still there is no response? Ask again. And if still there is no response? Communicate our feelings about receiving no response. Invite our partner to share his or her feelings and reactions. And if our partner refuses, will make no effort even to understand? Then we must face something it may be painful to face: our partner does not seem to be interested in our desires or even in communicating on the subject. If that is a fact, it needs to be faced squarely; we can consider whether or not a solution is possible, and, if not, whether or not we are willing to live with the problem. But no good purpose is served by being afraid to discover the truth.

Manipulation

Often, when we do not feel free to express our wants directly, we try to get them satisfied indirectly, by manipulative behavior, which, whether or not it succeeds in the short term, tends to alienate and antagonize our partner and to create distance rather than closeness and intimacy.

We deal here with one of the fundamental barriers to communication: the substitution of *manipulations* for honest expressions of thoughts, feelings, and desires.

If we are so insecure that we cannot believe honest expression will ever get us what we want, if we feel that only manipulations can work, inevitably we will sabotage our love relationships. Inevitably we will sabotage *all* our important relationships.

It needs to be stressed, of course, that no one can always give us what we want, no one can always respond to us just as we would like and just at the moment we would like. No one else exists for the satisfaction of our desires. And if we attempt to manipulate a partner into this role, either by playing for sympathy or by playing for guilt, all we will succeed in doing in the end is to stimulate resentment, regardless of whether or not our partner is maneuvered into complying with our immediate request.

Honest communication, therefore, has a great deal to do with our willingness and courage to be who we are, to show who we are, to own our thoughts, feelings, and desires—to give up self-concealment as a survival strategy. But we cannot relinquish an error we are unwilling to recognize. So what is needed is a leap— into honesty. Just as romantic love is not for children, so it is not for liars, or for cowards.

Honesty and courage serve the growth of romantic love. Dishonesty and cowardice inevitably subvert it.

None of the foregoing discussion implies that we are to blurt out indiscriminately every passing feeling, urge, impulse, desire, fantasy, and thought. Such a policy is neither possible nor advisable. I am concerned here with establishing, in a very general way, communication behaviors that serve romantic love and behaviors that subvert it. In applying these principles in practice, sensitivity, intelligence, an appreciation of specific contexts and situations is always required; the foregoing are not rules to be followed mechanically.

If, for example, we see that our partner is struggling with some weighty problem of his or her own, we may wisely hesitate to share certain of our thoughts or feelings at that time; we may wait till a later time or else choose to deal with them alone. Further, communication is rarely effective when unaccompanied by benevolence and respect, particularly in the context of romantic love; there is a difference between expressing wants simply, directly, and lovingly and expressing them with shrill, demanding hostility or resentment. And there will be times when we will see clearly that our partner is not in position to satisfy some of our wants and no good purpose is achieved by introducing reproach and guilt into the situation.

This said, the underlying truth remains: If we wish to understand why, with one couple, love seems to grow, and why, with another, love dies, it is instructive to watch how the woman and man talk to and relate to each other—how they communicate. There we will see an essential ingredient of the answer.

Projecting Visibility

It is clear that romantic love entails a desire to see and be seen, to appreciate and to be appreciated, to know and to be known, to explore and to be explored, to give visibility and to receive it. As discussed in Chapter 2, this is not an incidental feature of romantic love, but its core, its essence.

If we talk to people who have been happily in love for some time, we will often hear such statements as the following: "He (she) makes me feel appreciated." "He (she) makes me feel better understood than I've ever felt in my life." "He makes me feel like a woman." "She makes me feel *seen*."

If we watch two people who are in love, if we watch their eyes, we can notice how central *seeing* is to passionate love. The ability to see and to communicate what one sees—that is, the ability to make the partner feel visible—is essential to the longevity of a romantic relationship.

If we watch a couple who have grown tired of each other we will notice that they rarely look at each other, or rarely look in the sense of active seeing; there is dullness in their eyes, a blankness, as if something inside them had shut down.

For men and women who are not afraid to love, who are not obsessed with fear of rejection, one of the great pleasures of being in love is the pleasure of making the partner feel more visible to him- or herself, more self-aware and more self-appreciative. One of the great pleasures is to lead the partner to deeper and deeper levels of self-discovery.

Such an attitude originates in the fact of being truly *fascinated* with the partner, of *wanting* to see and understand this other human being, and of realizing that this is a process without end. Contrary to the cliché that "love is blind," love has the power of seeing with the greatest clarity and to the greatest depth, because the motivation is there, the inspiration is there. Those whom we do not love we do not ordinarily look at closely or for such long periods of time.

Sometimes I will hear a person say, "But I understand my partner totally. There is nothing new to see or discover. How could there be? We have been together for ten years!" A person who speaks in this manner is revealing something else entirely, not about the partner but about the self: an attitude of mental passivity that commonly is manifest in other areas of life as well. It is never true that there is "nothing more to understand." There is always more, if only because a person is engaged in a constant process of unfolding. And further, our active desire to *see* our partner and our ability to do so with fresh eyes *encourages* the process of growth and unfolding within him or her.

I am thinking of couples I know who have succeeded in sustaining love over long periods of time. Very commonly the two people will ask each other, "What do you think? What do you feel?" They will watch each other with genuine interest; they will lean forward with excitement, their eyes sparkling with awareness. They enjoy communicating what they see or sense about the other.

The excitement in their relationship is the reflection of an excitement existing within each of them as individuals. This excitement needs to be better understood because of its relevance to the sustaining of visibility in particular and romantic love in general.

Visibility and Excitement

Many people live automatically; they live off past thinking and past perceptions and past learnings. Hence life loses its freshness very early. Enthusiasm dies quickly. Passion dies quite soon. They have turned themselves more or less into machines and, as machines, they speak with great authority on the fact that inevitably passion is short-lived, as inevitably romantic love must die, as inevitably all enthusiasm must flag. Their delusion is that they are speaking about reality; the truth is that they are speaking about themselves.

It is often observed that creative people exhibit a childlike quality, a freshness and spontaneity in their way of perceiving and responding to life. The essence of creativity is *retaining* the capacity to see life afresh every day and therefore to be able to perceive the unexpected, to leap into the unfamiliar, to be open to the novel.

This is precisely the attitude that is required for the sustaining of passion—and for the continuing communication of visibility to the person one loves.

Observe that, for most people, it is not only that romantic love has died by the time they are in their thirties (or much earlier); virtually *all* their enthusiasms and passions have faded away. Why single out romantic love? It is not as if they had kept their other passions aflame and only romantic love has become extinguished. *They* have become extinguished.

The question is not must romantic love die? The question is must *all* excitement and enthusiasm die?

However we answer, we will be answering for ourselves. People who have become machines naturally insist that to be a machine is the essence of our humanity. But those who have not become automatons, those who perceive the world anew every day, those who delight in consciousness and in the activity of consciousness, can only listen to such statements of despair with incredulity. *Their* experience is different.

Of course, they are a minority. But they exist. And their existence is a living refutation of so much of the nonsense that is written on the subject of romantic love by self-proclaimed experts who lost the capacity to experience it very early, if they possessed it at all.

None of the foregoing is intended to refute the fact that romantic love tends to pass through stages, and that the tenth year of a relationship will obviously be experienced, in some respects, differently from the first. But I cannot resist mentioning that, as I was editing this section, a couple came to see me for counseling; during the session, even while airing disagreements, they could not keep their hands off each other; she was sixty-two years old, he was sixty-five.

"Excitement" is the felt energy that we experience flowing within us and that we have available for our responses. The enemy of excitement, and therefore of the ability to experience and express continuing appreciation of our partner, is emotional repression, self-disowning, self-alienation. People learn to turn against themselves, to "turn off" so as to avoid getting hurt or to win approval or status; they then complain of feelings of emptiness and futility and loss of passion.

Sometimes they decide that romantic love is "too narrowly selfish," that personal passion and excitement are "socially unimportant," or even "antisocial," and they try to discover a new source of aliveness and affiliation with some "great cause," a doctrine, an ideology, a movement, something "greater than themselves," something that promises them a substitute for selfhood and personal identity. They are incapable of loving a single human being, but they love "humanity" (Hoffer, 1951).

We stay alive, psychologically, by staying in touch with our feelings, with our emotions, with our thoughts and longings and fantasies and judgments—with everything that pertains to the world of our inner experience. And we keep our relationships alive by *sharing* this inner world, by *exposing* it, by *expressing* it, by making it part of the *lived reality* of our existence. And this includes, as an essential feature, remaining sensitive to what we see in our partner and to how he or she

affects us, the feelings and thoughts our partner inspires in us, all of which pertain to the issue of psychological visibility.

Relationships can starve to death through silence,
the absence of this flow of energy between two people,
the absence of exchanging the experience of visibility.
This is one of the reasons why it is so important to
express one's feelings when we are hurt or angry. If we
fail to do so, after a time we bury more than hurt and
anger; love and appreciation tend to be submerged as
well. We become silent, withdrawn, remote. In supress-
ing negative feelings, we also disown positive ones,
building a protective wall of indifference. Our partner
is now experienced not as a source of pleasure but as a
source of pain against which we protect ourselves by
numbness. We "shut down," refuse to give our partner
the pleasure of feeling visible and appreciated. But
then where does our relationship go from there? It
becomes a dead end.

We all know that nothing gives us the experience of
being loved as much as when we feel that we are a
source of joy to our partner. There is very little nourishment in a dispassionate analysis of our "virtues," or
in compliments so sweeping and general that they have
no specific meaning or emotional charge. But the smile
of pleasure on our partner's face when we enter the
room, a glance of admiration aimed at something we
have done, an expression of sexual desire or excitement, an interest in what we are thinking or feeling, a
recognition of what we are thinking or feeling even
when we have not explained, a conveyed sense of joy
from being in contact with us or simply from watching
us—these are the means by which the experience of
visibility and of being loved are created, are made real
to us. And these are the means by which we create the
experience for our partner.

Fear of Excitement

Can anything be more inspiring than to allow our
partner to see the excitement that he or she stimulates

in us? Unfortunately, many of us were raised to conceal such excitement, to subdue and submerge it, to extinguish it in order to appear grown up—so we are afraid to let our partner see how much we feel, how much love radiates through us, how much pleasure our mate can inspire.

Or perhaps we *want* to express it, we *want* to communicate it, and it is our partner who withdraws, who turns us off, who signals that such messages are better left uncommunicated, because our partner is made anxious by excitement, even by the excitement that he or she ignites.

But fear of excitement kills romantic love.

During my Intensives I sometimes take a group through a simple exercise. Students are asked to close their eyes and imagine themselves as children playing alone, feeling happy and joyous and filled with energy, and then to imagine first Mother and then Father entering the scene, and then to notice what happens physically, to notice what happens on a body level, to notice what happens to their breathing, to their feelings, to their emotions.

The majority report a tensing, a shutting down, a relinquishing of their excitement. The majority report that Mother and Father are experienced as *the enemy of their excitement*. They become aware of the extent to which they have learned to suppress or repress excitement as a matter of course, to treat it almost as a shameful secret not to be shared or exposed.

I will sometimes say to the group, *"Never marry a person who is not a friend of your excitement."* If our partner is not comfortable with excitement, in the end he or she will not be comfortable with love, even the love we feel for him or her. And if we do not feel that our partner is the friend of our excitement, then no matter how much he or she may profess to love us, we cannot feel fully visible, we cannot feel fully loved, we cannot feel fully accepted—and we cannot even feel that our love for our partner is fully accepted.

As I have repeatedly stressed, our partner's manner

of treating us is only a reflection of the manner of treating him- or herself, just as our manner of treating our partner is only a reflection of our manner of treating ourselves. If we cannot accept the excitement within ourselves, if we do not feel free to show it, how can we hope to do better by the excitement in anyone else?

One of my happiest memories of Patrecia is of the look on her face when she would come to collect me at the airport when I returned from a trip—a look of eagerness, expectancy, and enchantment, as if something wonderful were in the process of happening. It was a special look, more eloquent than words. Seeing that look, it was impossible not to feel visible, impossible not to feel loved. She was not afraid to experience her excitement or show it. It was her greatest gift. And that energy joins with mine in the writing of this book.

Interlude: An Experiment in Intimacy

We have been discussing mutual self-disclosure and the art of communication, both of which are vital to the creation of that quality of *intimacy* between a man and a woman which romantic love requires. Intimacy pertains to the sharing of the self on the deepest and most personal and private level—an "exchange of vulnerabilities," in the words of Masters and Johnson (1970). I should like to pause here to report on what I have called "an experiment in intimacy" that I sometimes suggest in the course of my work with couples.

Sometimes, when working with a man and woman who have become estranged from each other or whose relationship appears to have become lifeless and mechanical, I will propose a certain "homework assignment." They are asked to spend a day together, entirely alone. No books, no television, no telephone calls. If they have children they make arrangements for someone to take care of them. No distractions of any kind are allowed. They are committed to remaining in the same room with each other for twelve hours. They further agree that no matter what the other might say, neither will leave the room refusing to talk. And of course there must under no circumstances be any physical violence. They can sit for several hours in total and absolute silence if they like, but they must remain together.

Typically, in the first hour or two there is some stiffness, there is self-consciousness; there may be joking or sparks of irritation. But almost always, after awhile, communication begins. Perhaps one partner talks about something that has angered him or her. Perhaps a quarrel develops. But then, within another hour or two, the situation begins to reverse itself; there is growing closeness, a new intimacy. Very often they make love. Afterward they are generally cheerful and, although it may be only three o'clock in the afternoon, one of them, out of nervousness, frequently proposes that the experiment has "worked" so it is all right now to go off to the movies or take a drive or visit friends or *do something*. But if they stay with their original commitment, which of course they are urged to do, they soon move down to a much deeper level of contact and intimacy than the earlier one, and the area of communication begins to expand. Often they share feelings they have never discussed before—talk of dreams and longings that they have never revealed before. They discover things in themselves and their partner that they have never realized before. They are free during this twelve-hour session to talk about anything, *providing it is personal,* as opposed to discussions of business, problems concerning the children's schoolwork, domestic details, and so forth. They must talk about themselves or each other or the relationship. Having placed themselves in a situation where all other sources of stimulation are absent, they have only their own selves and each other, and then they begin to learn the meaning of intimacy. There is almost always a gradual deepening of feeling, a deepening emotional involvement, an expanding experience of aliveness.

More often than not the day ends happily. But

sometimes it ends with the realization that the relationship may no longer serve the needs of either and that they may not wish to remain together. This is not a failure of the experiment, but a success. It is a success because the waste of two lives in an empty marriage or relationship is a tragedy.

When I first propose this experiment to couples I receive one of two reactions, generally speaking: anticipatory excitement—or anxiety. Either reaction is informative. If the thought of spending twelve hours in the presence of "only my mate" fills one with apprehension, that is a fact worth knowing.

I have found that for two people who love each other but who do not know how to make their relationship work, or do not seem to know how to communicate effectively, a twelve-hour session of this kind, participated in at least once a month, can produce the most radical changes in the quality of the relationship. One of the changes is the unexpected discovery of communication skills they did not even dream they could possess.

If a human being is always on the run, always engaged in "doing something," he or she has little or no chance for self-encounter and self-exploration. We need times of stillness to enter into ourselves, to experience who we are, to revitalize ourselves. The same thing is true of two people in a relationship. A relationship needs time, *it needs leisure*.

A couple may run from the tennis court to the bridge table to the Saturday night dance at their club, and insist that they are truly sharing a life, and not notice that they spend no time *encountering* each other. They are together, but they never meet.

It is generally recognized that creativity requires leisure, an absence of rush, time for the mind and imagination to float and wander and roam, time for the individual to descend into the depths of his or her psyche, to be available to the barely audible signals rustling for attention. Long periods of time may pass in which nothing seems to be happening. But we know that that kind of space must be created if the mind is to leap out of its accustomed ruts, to part from the mechanical, the known, the familiar, the standard, and generate a leap into the new.

Something very similar happens when a couple create a time and space for themselves without the distraction of any routine activities, so they can sit together, sometimes not talking, sometimes thinking aloud, permitting their thoughts and fantasies to lead them, slowly going deeper and deeper into who they are and what they feel and what they mean to each other. Hovering on the edges of the situation, there may be the risk of boredom; perhaps nothing will happen today; perhaps they will just sit, with seemingly endless time stretching out before them. The risk is necessary, just as it is necessary for one who creates. A person who schedules every moment of the day out of fear of ever being bored or having nothing to do is condemned to living on the surface of his or her mind, living superficially, living mechanically, living off the known and the familiar, because the new resides in the depths and, for entry into the depths, time without activity is needed.

Of course there is another risk involved: the risk of discovering things about each other, or about their own feelings, that they had been afraid to know. There are relationships that manage to survive only by virtue of what the couple have agreed not to talk about, never to discuss; for such couples intimacy and time spent alone together is a threat. In all unhappy relationships, where the couple choose to go on living together, there is a tacit agreement about that which is not to be discussed, not to be mentioned, not to be faced or acknowledged—such as how the man or woman feels about the quality of their sex life, or about what one or the other does when away alone on trips, or about how one feels about some habit of the other, and so forth. Such relationships are characterized by a quality of emotional deadness. When a couple in such a relationship agrees to participate in the "experiment in intimacy" I propose, there is often considerable apprehension that everything will blow up in their faces because they will no longer be able to avoid discussing what they have agreed not to discuss. And when they spend twelve hours together, often they do begin moving into the forbidden area, sometimes with surprising results. Contrary to their fears, the relationship is not destroyed, it is revitalized, often accompanied by needed changes in their respective behaviors.

When couples who do not spend time together in this manner, or who refuse to do so, hear of another couple who does, they sometimes respond by saying, "Well, it's easy for them to do it because they find each other very interesting." But it is no less true to say that the people find each other interesting precisely *because* they spend time together in this manner: *the method forbids them to live mechanically.**

In my experience, the results are often far more powerful than those achieved through marriage counseling.

I trust it is clear that the time span need not be twelve hours. Sometimes it can be longer, sometimes shorter. But here is what will *not* work: A man rushes home from the office, sits down opposite his wife in the living room, looks at his watch and says, "All right, we don't have to start dressing for the club for half an hour. Let's talk intimately. What do you want to say?"

There is no aphrodisiac in the world so powerful and, in the end, so reliable, as authentic communication that flows from the core of one being to the core of another. This, incidentally, is one of the reasons couples often find sex unusually exciting after a screaming fight. They have broken their mechanical pattern of relating. But there are other and better forms of intimacy than screaming fights. Fights have their uses, true enough, but as a steady diet or as an exclusive form of contact they do not provide much

---

*For couples who have troubles in their relationship, I generally suggest that they agree to from four to six such all-day sessions, at intervals of once a month.

nourishment. We should not need the force of anger to break down our walls. We should master the art of shattering them ourselves, if we wish to participate in romantic love.

Once, following a lecture in which I was discussing some of these issues, a couple came over to me, very enthusiastic about the talk, and proceeded to tell me how happily in love they were—which was how they looked. Then the man said to me, "But there's one thing that troubles me. *How do you find the time for that intimacy?*" I asked him what his profession was and he told me he was a lawyer. I said, "There's one thing that troubles me. Given how much in love you are with your wife, and looking at you both it seems clear that you are, *how do you find the time to attend to your law practice?*" He looked disoriented and nonplussed, as if the question were one he could not even grasp. "The question is incomprehensible, isn't it?" I said to him. "I mean, you *have to* attend to your law practice, don't you?—*that's important.*" Slowly a light began to dawn in his face. I went on, "Well, when and if you decide that love really matters to you as much as your work, when success in your relationship with this woman becomes as much an imperative as success in your career, you won't ask: *How does one find time?* You'll know how one does it."

I wish it were possible for me to claim that this last is a principle I have always understood. It isn't. When we are young we are so often reckless with life, reckless with love. We imagine that we, and those we love, will live forever. If, at times, we are neglectful of love, fail to be sufficiently nourishing to our partner because we are involved in our work, or some other activity, we tell ourselves, "Later. I'll take care of it later." Patrecia and I probably spent a good deal more time alone together than most couples, but still . . . I think of the times we could have been together and weren't, because I was doing something else, and I try to remember what it was that seemed so important at the time. It is not one of my happier memories.

In my observation the biggest time-threat comes, not from our work, but from our social relationships or what we tell ourselves are our social obligations. Often it is against these that love needs to be protected. The time that we and our partner spend in the company of friends or colleagues can be a source of pleasure, but it is not a substitute for time spent alone together. Nothing is. Evenings spent with people who do not matter to us, or do not matter nearly as much as the one we love, cannot be reclaimed at a later date, cannot be taken back and relived. It is now or never.

Sometimes, when counseling people who seem genuinely to be in love and yet who seem to be reckless with their relationship and unmindful of time, I want to cry out to them, "We are not immortal! Don't assume you will have all the time you need! None of us knows who will still be here next week! *Be here now! Let your love happen now!*"

The Art of Nurturing

Virtually all of the qualities and attitudes needed for the fulfillment of romantic love require maturity; this can hardly be stressed enough. If we can see only our own needs and not the needs of our partner, we are in the relation of a child to a parent, not of an equal to an equal. In romantic love, independent equals do not drain each other; they nurture each other.

To nurture another human being, in the sense meant here, is to accept him or her unreservedly; to respect his or her sovereignty and integrity; to support his or her growth and self-actualization needs; and to *care*, on the deepest and most intimate level, about his or her thoughts, feelings, and wants. It is to create a context and environment in which a person can live and flourish.

To nurture another human being means to accept that person as he or she is, and yet to believe in possibilities within that person still unrealized. It is to be honest with that person about our own needs and wants, and always to remember that the other person does not exist merely to satisfy our needs and wants. It means to express confidence in the person's strengths and internal resources, and yet be available to offer help when it is asked for (and sometimes to recognize that it might be needed even when it is not being asked for). It is to create a context in which the person can experience that he or she *matters,* that the expression of thoughts and feelings will be welcomed, and yet to understand that there are times when what our partner needs is silence and aloneness.

To nurture is to caress and stroke, without making demands; to hold and protect; to allow tears and to offer comfort; to fetch a cup of tea or coffee unasked.

Without any implication of immaturity, there exists in each one of us the child we once were, and there are times when that child too needs nurturing. We need to be aware of the child in ourselves and in our partner. We need to be in good relationship with that child. To nurture someone we love is to nurture the child within that adult person, and to accept that child as a valid part of who that person is. To nurture is to love not only our partner's strength but also his or her fragility, not only that within our partner which is powerful but also that which is delicate.

It is just this pattern of mutual caring and nurturing that we can observe between men and women who love each other and who know how to love. Out of the fullness of their own being comes their ability to nurture. Out of their sensitivity to their own needs, they are sensitive to the needs of their partner. Out of acceptance of the child in the self, comes acceptance of the child in the partner. It is easy enough to understand why for such persons love grows.

And it is easy enough to understand why, in the absence of such understanding and such nurturing, love tends to diminish, dry up, and die.

To be nurtured is to experience that I am cared for. Not to be nurtured is to be deprived of the experience that I am cared for.

I am thinking of a couple I know who are very much in love and very immature, the woman in particular. Their relationship is tense and stormy, filled with passion, tears, separations, and reunions. There are many reasons for their conflict but one clearly has to do with the woman's inability to nurture. Not that she is callous or indifferent; not that she does not try. She cares and does try; she thinks she does "all the right things" and cannot understand why her man is unsatisfied and unfulfilled. She "plays" at being nurturing, going through some of the motions as conscientiously as she can: *See what a good girl I am? Now will you take care of me?* The nurturing she offers is not organic, it does not come from her core, and the man senses this, even if he cannot put his feelings into words. It does not come out of the spontaneous fullness of love or the spontaneous fullness of self. And it is subtly manipulative, although I doubt that the woman is aware of this, in the ordinary meaning of awareness.

It sometimes happens that men and women who genuinely do love each other fail to be nurturing. In addition to what I have already said, the following considerations seem relevant. If we do not have a fairly solid level of self-esteem, it will not be all that real to us that what we do matters to another human being, one way or the other; we will not feel that effective; we will not be aware of our ability to have an impact upon another person—and consequently we can fail to know that we have the *power* to nurture the person we love. Or, even if we do know it, out of an accumulation of past hurts and resentments undealt with, we may be emotionally blocked with our partner in ways that inhibit the flow of feeling and energy that nurturing entails. Or, after years of frustration, we may have disowned and repressed our own need and desire for nurturing and, in consequence, are out of touch with that need in our partner. For example, in my observation and experience, men and women who are insensitive to moments when their partner needs to be held and stroked are often oblivious to their own needs to be held and stroked. Whatever the reasons why a man and woman may fail to nuture each other, there is no way for love not to suffer.

Returning to the "good girl" of the preceding story, for example, it is not that she is too "selfish." Far from it. It is that her self is too undeveloped, too immature. There are, after all, limits to how nurturing a child can be.

Indeed, if she were to try to be "unselfish," the problem would only be compounded. Her man would have reason to feel still more resentment. We do not want to be nurtured as an act of self-sacrifice. We want to feel that our partner is selfishly invested in the act of nurturing. The woman's problem is not that she is "selfish" but that her selfishness does not include and embrace her partner, which is precisely what does happen in mature love.

The concept of selfishness is so central to mature, romantic love that we shall take a moment to clarify it further.

Love and Selfishness

Of all the nonsense written about love, none is more absurd than the notion that ideal love is *selfless*. What I love is the embodiment of my values in another person; properly understood, love is a profound act of *self-assertion*.

To love *selfishly* does not mean to be indifferent to the needs or interests of the partner. To say it once more: When we love, our concept of our self-interest expands to embrace the well-being of our partner. That is the great compliment of love: to declare to another human being that his or her happiness is of *selfish* importance to ourselves.

It would hardly be a compliment to tell a person we love that his or her well-being and happiness are *not* of selfish interest to us. To love is to see myself in you and to wish to celebrate myself with you; this is hardly unselfish. Yet it is the very essence of love.

If I accept and respect you, it is not selfless. If I honor your integrity, it is not selfless. If I care about your thoughts and feelings, if I hold you in my arms, if I stroke and caress you, if I love you as I love my own life—it is not selfless.

And when we who are in love have the wisdom to spend time together alone . . . doing nothing as the word *doing* is ordinarily understood . . . just being together, just sharing our beings, sharing our thoughts, our feelings, our fantasies, our longings . . . sharing the voyage into that self, using each other to go deeper and deeper into that self, using each other as a guide, a facilitator, a mirror, a sounding board for the exploration of the self . . . making of love a pathway to self-discovery, making of love a vehicle for personal growth, making of love a doorway to personal evolution—is this not the noblest and most exalted expression of intelligent selfishness?

To love *selflessly* is a contradiction in terms.

To help us understand this, let us ask ourselves whether we want our lover to caress us *un*selfishly, with no personal gratification in the doing, or do we want our lover to caress us because it is a joy and a pleasure for him or her to do so? And let us ask ourselves whether we want our partner to spend time with us, alone together, and to experience the doing as an *act of self-sacrifice?* Or do we want our partner to experience such time as glory? And if it is glory that we want our partner to feel, if we want our partner to experience joy in our presence, excitement in our being, ardor, passion, fascination, delight, then let us stop talking of "selfless love" as a noble ideal.

Even in the most intimate and loving of relationships, we need to be aware of and to respect our own needs and wants. Not that compromise and accommodation have no place in a love relationship; obviously they have. But if too often I ignore or sacrifice my own needs and wants in order to please or satisfy you, I commit a crime against both of us: against myself, because of the treason I commit to my own values—

and to you, because in allowing you to be the collector of my sacrificial offerings I am allowing you to become someone I will resent. Love is hardly served by such a policy.

If we see a person who professes to love but does not understand the art of nourishing, as discussed above, that person's problem is one not of "selfishness" but of immaturity. It is not self-sacrifice that romantic love requires, but a grown-up's understanding of selfishness.

Sex as an Expression of Love

Sometimes, when we think about the challenges of romantic love, think about all the hurdles that have to be met and crossed, it is difficult not to feel sadness— sadness for every couple who has ever fallen in love, and then helplessly watched while love slipped away and they did not know how to stop it, did not know what had happened or why.

Sometimes it is easy enough to see where people are being irresponsible or willfully and perversely unconscious or petulantly childish, and then, perhaps, we do not feel a great deal of sympathy. But when the causes of love's disintegration are subtler, less transparent, and the couple's bewilderment more authentic, then we can hardly help but feel the pain of all those who struggle in the dark to create a life for themselves.

I am thinking of those who grew up alienated from their own sexuality, those who experience their sexual responses, fantasies, and behavior as something disquietingly foreign, not an organic and natural expression of the self. For them love can be very difficult because their desires do not follow the pathway of their admiration, do not follow the pathway of their professed values, but take their orders from a different source, a self that has never matured.

We recognize, of course, that sex and love, though related, are obviously different. We recognize that sexual desire does not necessarily entail love. We recognize that gratifying sexual experiences can occur without great love. That is not the point. We recognize also that the greatest and most intense sexual experiences occur in the context of love, occur as an expression of love. What is the torment, then, of those who claim that when they feel love they do not necessarily feel ardent desire, or who claim that their best sexual experiences take place when "unencumbered" by love? These are the sexually self-alienated men and women whose love lives are inevitably unsatisfying. Sometimes their "solution" is to declare with casual indifference that they are not really interested in love, that it "gets in the way."

We need to remember that sexual self-alienation, like every form of self-alienation, is a state of mind. By this I mean that, *in fact,* our sexual responses are *always* an expression of the self, *always* an expression of who we are, but that is not necessarily how we experience them.

It is generally recognized that antisexual messages absorbed in childhood from parents and religious teachers encourage and exacerbate sexual self-alienation. The tendency then is to view sex as the darker and least acceptable side of the self. But of course sexual self-alienation can have many roots.

When we enjoy healthy self-esteem, when we feel love of ourself and in harmony with ourself, then sex is a natural and spontaneous expression of our feelings for our partner, for ourself, and for life. But when we are deeply insecure about our worth, when we live with the chronic sense of feeling threatened or doomed, sex can become a means of proving we are "bad," just as Mummy or Daddy said, of reassuring ourselves that we are *not* "bad," of controlling another human being and thus proving we are "safe," of reconnecting in unconscious fantasy with Mother or Father, and so forth.

The bed is like a metaphysical arena in which we play out the basic drama of our existence. We know, for example, that a high proportion of persons who are strongly preoccupied with power—more particularly with political power—are inclined to reach their greatest peaks of sexual intensity in sadomasochistic experiences (see Janus, Bess, and Saltus, 1977). Pain—the ability to inflict pain and/or to endure pain—is at a very high emotional premium. Rarely are such persons' best sex with their marriage partner; they generally do not feel free to explore the depths of their fascination with pain, humiliation, and degradation in that context; often, prostitutes serve their purpose better.

Bed can be a place where we play out our fear of intimacy, so that sex never truly rises above the level of masturbation. Bed can be the place where two children hold hands against the mysterious terrors of the adult world. Bed can be the place where a man or woman endlessly reenacts the struggle to gain the love and approval of a rejecting parent.

Bed can also be the place where an individual's love affair with life explodes and overflows in a torrent of joy and excitement. Bed can be a place in which two lovers, in the act of worshiping each other, overflow the boundaries of flesh and spirit and make manifest the deepest values of their existence.

What successful romantic love requires is a sexuality that is integrated with the self, that is not experienced as being at war with other cardinal values of the self.

If we are not divided against ourselves, if we are not engaged in a constant struggle to "prove" our worth or to "prove" anything, then we are free to enjoy our own being, to enjoy the state of being alive, to enjoy and appreciate our partner; we do not experience a split between mind and body, between spirit and flesh, between admiration and passion. Then we truly think and feel that our partner is wonderful; we take pride in the direction of our sexual desires.

The trouble is that if we do not like our particular sexual responses, we are inclined to disown them even while acting on them, to deny or avoid the reality of what we are feeling and what we are doing, and thus to keep our sexual psychology hermetically sealed, cut off from the rest of our conscious experience, cut off from our knowledge and intelligence, and so we remain helplessly stuck, *unnecessarily* stuck. We cannot hope to outgrow a condition whose reality we will not own, will not accept, will not allow ourselves to experience fully. And so we remain the prisoner of our immaturity, of the unfinished business of our childhood, which keeps us from the joys and gratifications of adulthood.

In this trapped state, romantic love can be felt only as a painful longing for a distant, unattainable ideal, possible, perhaps, to others, but never to oneself.

So we can appreciate how preciously valuable is an attitude of guiltless and joyous acceptance of sex and of one's own sexual feelings and responses, and of one's own body and of the body of the opposite gender.

When sex is experienced not as a source of shame or guilt, but as a vehicle for self-worship and for the worship of our partner, when sex is experienced as an expression of our aliveness, of our joy in being, then a major road has been opened to the fulfillment of romantic love.

Through the giving and receiving of sexual pleasure lovers continually reaffirm that they are a source of joy to each other. Joy is a nutrient of love: it makes love grow. On the other hand, it is very difficult not to experience sexual neglect as rejection or abandonment, no matter what the partner's other protestations of devotion. No, sex is not all there is to romantic love; but can one imagine fulfilled romantic love without it? Perhaps under very unusual, very tragic circumstances; but never as a preferred way of life. Sex at its highest potential is the ultimate celebration of love.

Admiration

While acknowledging the importance of sexual passion, the fact remains that sexual passion alone cannot sustain a couple across a lifetime, cannot provide a sufficient support for all the weight a relationship must carry. Only admiration can do that.

Throughout the preceding discussion there is the clear implication that the two people in a love relationship admire each other. Unfortunately, this is not always the case. But what is the case is that, in the absence of admiration, it is extraordinarily difficult for romantic love to survive the stresses to which it inevitably is subject.

The admiration between two people is the most powerful support system a relationship can have, the most powerful foundation. Consequently there is the greatest likelihood that the couple will be able to handle the pressures and weather the storms that inevitably are a part of life and, therefore, sooner or later part of every relationship.

For many people it is frightening to ask, "Do I admire my partner?" It seems less frightening to ask, "Do I love my partner? Do I desire my partner? Do I have a pleasant time with my partner?" To ask, "Do I admire my partner?" is to risk discovering that I may be bound to him or her more through dependency than admiration, more through immaturity or fear or "convenience" than genuine esteem.

Whenever I raise the subject of admiration in the context of romantic love at a public lecture, it seems to me that I can almost literally see a ripple of apprehension moving through various couples in the room. On the positive side, it must be stressed, there are couples who visibly beam with pleasure and pride when the subject is raised.

What is odd is how unconscious many people keep themselves concerning the importance of this issue. They can talk for hours about the difficulties in their relationship and never think to raise this question.

I remember once a woman came for a consultation because she was unhappy with her husband. She professed to be bewildered as to the reason. I asked her what kind of man her husband was and what she thought of him. She answered, "He is marvelous. He brings me breakfast in bed every morning. He is very kind, never criticizing, never complaining, never demanding. He is thoughtful in every possible way. I've never been treated so well in my life. He is wonderful." I said, "But aside from that, aside from how he treats you, how do you see him as a human being?" She answered spontaneously, "He's terrible. A liar. A weakling. Right now he's embezzling money from the firm where he works. He lives off his charm. He's— he's a great big nothing!" When I gently inquired as to whether any of that could be relevant to her feelings of unhappiness, she looked as if she were the sudden recipient of a miraculously profound revelation.

Any number of internal or external pressures may cause our love to falter, during the long course of a relationship, on just about any of the virtues described in this chapter; admiration may sustain a relationship when this happens. Where admiration is lacking, we far less easily tolerate what we perceive to be our partner's defects. Besides providing support in the middle of a storm, however, admiration is enriching in many ways. In receiving admiration we feel visible, appreciated, loved, and thus reinforced in our love for our partner. In experiencing and expressing admiration, we feel pride in our choice of mate, confirmed in our judgment, and strengthened in our feelings of love. Two lovers who profoundly admire each other know a form of delight that is a continuing source of fuel to romantic love.

Which leads us back to the beginning of this chapter: the importance of self-esteem. When high-self-esteem people fall in love, admiration is most likely to be at the core of their relationship. They are most likely to admire and to be admired. Admiration does not figure prominently in relationships between people with low self-esteem. Indeed, in my experience the question of admiration is one they generally prefer not to hear raised.

Small wonder that when a man and woman admire

each other, love tends to grow. Small wonder that when they don't, love tends to die.

The Courage to Love

When people discuss the challenges and difficulties of romantic love there is an issue they rarely mention: Romantic love can be terrifying.

When we fall in love we experience another human being as enormously important to us, enormously important to our personal happiness. We allow that person to enter the private world within us, which, perhaps, no one else has ever entered or even known about. So there is a surrender, not a surrender to the other person so much as to our feeling *for* the other person. Without that surrender love is aborted at the outset.

In allowing another human being to become so vitally important to us, what is the problem? What is the obstacle? Very simply, it lies in the possibility of loss. It lies in the possibility of the other person's not loving us in return. Or falling out of love with us. Or dying.

In my Intensive on *Self-Esteem and Romantic Relationships,* I ask students to break up into small groups, with men and women separated, and to explore their feelings about needing the opposite sex. It is very common for participants to get in touch with feelings not only of fear but also of anger, of resentment: Need creates a vulnerability that can be frightening—and enraging.

In my experience a great deal of the so-called war of the sexes is a result of a fear of rejection, abandonment, or loss. Often men and women experience great resistance to owning how much they need each other, how important the opposite sex is for the enjoyment of life and the fulfillment of their own masculine or feminine potentialities. Often there is almost hatred of the fact that we need the opposite sex as much as we do.

I am convinced that a great many of the foolish things women say about men and men say about women in moments of hurt, suspiciousness, or anger are merely the product and reflection of past painful experiences of rejection or abandonment. There is a tendency not to own the fear, not to face it honestly, not to recognize it for what it is, but to rationalize it, to justify it in terms of sweeping generalizations about "men" or "women," to avoid confronting the anxiety and hurt that is at the real root of such talk.

Since most people have already experienced painful feelings of rejection in childhood they are, in effect, "primed" for catastrophe, "primed" for tragedy when, as adults, they fall in love. They "know" that love means pain, hurt, nonacceptance, loss. In addition to childhood experiences they may have been emotionally bruised or battered in earlier love affairs. So they "know" that love means torment.

Earlier I spoke about the importance of communication. But this fear is itself a massive barrier to communication. When a couple in love quarrel it is very common to see each of them "shut down," disconnect from the depth of their feelings for each other, disconnect from the depth of their love, so as to protect themselves in case things don't work out. They become impersonal, remote, even hostile. They are afraid but they do not acknowledge that they are afraid; instead, they throw up defenses, throw up barriers. They do not remain open and vulnerable. In consequence, communication is blocked, sabotaged. When they talk they rarely express what they are actually feeling. Their communications are a distortion because their deepest feelings are forbidden expression. This is why the resolution of conflicts can be so difficult. They do not talk to each other from their core; they talk from behind their masks.

Many men carry within them conscious or unconscious feelings of hostility toward women and many women carry within them conscious or unconscious feelings of hostility toward men. This is not—and cannot be—in the nature of life. Men and women need each other. That should make them friends. Instead, too often, it makes them enemies because of the fear and anticipation of being hurt.

It is not the fear as such that causes the damage, but the denial of the fear, the refusal to own it and to deal with it honestly. Each senses this hostility in the other, and his or her own fear and hostility are subsequently reinforced. If it is a love affair, it is a love affair between two fortresses.

When there is trouble between them the man or woman does not say, "I love you and I am frightened of losing you." He or she says, "I am no longer so sure I love you." It takes courage to say, "I'm afraid." When they lack this courage the price often paid is the destruction of a relationship. And when, through cowardice, they have wrecked several relationships they are more than ready for those who will tell them that romantic love is an immature delusion. Better to blame romantic love than to acknowledge that it is not a game for the frail of heart.

Sometimes I have heard a man or a woman discuss their fear of romantic love, not in terms of rejection or abandonment, but in terms of the loss of self. There is the fear that romantic love will necessitate a surrender of personal identity, a fear, in effect, that they will be taken over, body and soul, by their lover. I have never heard this fear expressed (with full seriousness) by a man or a woman with a high level of self-esteem and a strong sense of personal autonomy. On the contrary: In my experience it is precisely men and women who are self-assured and self-confident who exhibit least anxiety in surrendering to love. My sense is that people who speak of fearing the loss of self, in this context, are unwittingly acknowledging the intensity of their longing for love, of their craving for love and their fear that in order to obtain it they will sacrifice anything, their mind, their values, their integrity. If this is true then the problem lies in inadequate autonomy, in an underdeveloped personal identity, and not in the nature of love.

Sometimes I have had a man or woman speak of love as a threat to their work. To surrender to love, they say, is to undermine their total commitment to their careers. As a man who has been achievement-oriented all his life and who knows rather a lot about what it means to love his work, I have never for a moment believed this argument. I am convinced it is a rationalization for fear of intimacy. Sometimes there is the additional fear that the lover will not respect their work needs and that out of fear of displeasing the lover they will no longer give work its due. This is very much like the problem of the person who speaks about loss of self. It is a problem of inadequate self-assertion, inadequate autonomy. It is a problem of inadequate maturity. Of course, if a person has this problem and does not know how to resolve it, it is better that he or she face that fact consciously and not attempt intimate relationships. But this is rarely what such persons choose to do. They want love, they want relationships, they want marriage, but they do not want that which is logically entailed by a serious commitment: They do not want the obligation to carry their own weight, they do not want to be there, in the relationship, except at unpredictable moments, and they want their partner to accept that, to absorb it uncomplainingly, and to support the pretense that they have a romance. What they want, then, is a contradiction: to be in love and yet not to be in love.

But even if we have made none of these mistakes, even if we have not suffered from rejection in childhood or in past love affairs, even if we do not approach love with any of the fears or misgivings I have described, there is still one ultimate threat that must be acknowledged: the loss of our loved one through death. As a possibility, this is, after all, in the very nature of our existence. Someone has to die first. And we cannot know when. We do not have to torment ourselves with this realization, but we can hardly avoid the knowledge that the issue exists. And even if we have the wisdom to accept it serenely, still we must face it first, acknowledge it, look at it. And for this, clarity is needed, honesty is needed—courage is needed.

When, during my agony over Patrecia's death, I found myself falling in love with another woman, the terror that I sometimes felt is truly indescribable. I was forced to confront, at the deepest level, the most fearsome aspect of romantic love.

I have spoken earlier about the art of accepting one's feelings, the art of not fighting reality, of flowing with one's experience. There is never a time when our understanding of this principle is more severely tested than when we must deal with the loss of a loved one through death. Mourning is necessary, grieving is necessary if the organism is to recover, if emotional well-being is ever again to be possible. But it is a process terrible beyond words.

It is not simply a matter of allowing pain to be felt. It is a matter of being willing to experience *everything*, of accepting without censorship and without self-reproach all the feelings, thoughts, fantasies that arise to torment one at such times.

To make the full reality of the situation clear I need to say something about what life was like the year following Patrecia's death.

On some days, or during some moments or hours, I would feel the horror of the accident and the loss rising within me and I would feel my body involuntarily tensing against the agony and I would tell myself, "Breathe. Don't fight. Accept." Sometimes I would feel myself assailed by guilt and self-reproach and I would not attempt to argue that this was irrational. I would tell myself, "Fine. Today is your day to feel guilty. Accept this, too." On some mornings I would awaken feeling unaccountably euphoric and then, minutes or hours later, the euphoria would turn into tears and then into animal wails; there was nothing to be done but accept all of it, not to fight but to allow, to permit the organism to do whatever it needed to do, to experience whatever it needed to experience. Sometimes, at unpredictable moments, there were violent sexual feelings—then violent rage—then, at other times, a devastating sense of powerlessness. There were days when I would find myself recalling every bit of Patrecia's behavior that had ever bothered me, as if by focusing on real or imagined faults I could thereby minimize the magnitude of the loss. I tried not to fight, I tried not to change or correct anything. I simply allowed, watched, and waited. Worst of all, perhaps, were the times when everything inside me seemed to be disintegrating, as if the entire structure of my mind and body were crumbling and I was falling endlessly through space. I could hear every cell in my body screaming Patrecia's name.

Of course there were times when I did fight against feeling what I was feeling, times when I did resist, times when it all became too much and my whole body contracted into one immense "No!" Then the challenge became to *accept the resistance,* to allow the fighting and the denial, to experience that—and to wait.

It was an act of trust, trust in the organism's powers of self-repair, trust that if I did my best not to disown my experience and to own my moments of disowning when they did occur, eventually a healing integration would happen. This is what has happened—and what continues to happen.

But, in the throes of all this, to open myself to another woman, to allow another human being to matter, to matter all the way down, to matter without reservation or restraint, meant, in principle, to make myself once again vulnerable to this kind of agony, at some unknown point in the future, to the possibility of it. It was in this manner that I had to confront the worst terror of romantic love.*

I have been very fortunate. The woman with whom I have fallen in love encourages me to speak about and

---

*Sometimes something of this terror is experienced when a person falls in love again, not after a death but after an excruciatingly painful divorce. The principle—and the problem—are the same.

share not only my feelings of anxiety about falling in love again but also all the feelings I experience relative to Patrecia. I have never had to hide or conceal anything.

What are we to do when and if we feel the terror I am describing? We own it. We express it. We talk about it. We do not pretend it does not exist.

It is not the fear of loss that destroys us. It is denying the fear. If we own it, if we express it, we discover that gradually it disappears. And even when it is still present it does not manipulate us into behaving in ways that sabotage love. But if we make ourselves unconscious of it, if we deny it, then we become its unwitting pawn and we find ourselves mysteriously withdrawing from our partner or become inappropriately critical or wondering if we do not perhaps long for our freedom, or practicing some other maneuver that will subvert our happiness.

Unconsciousness is always the enemy—and consciousness is always the solution. The solution is awareness, acceptance, expression.

I said at the start that I see romantic love as one of the great challenges and one of the great adventures of our existence. It requires much of us. It demands a high level of personal evolution. And it is pitiless—like the law of gravity. If we are not ready, we fall. If we are not ready, we fail.

But even if we fulfill the requirements of love, we wonder whether or not it will last forever. We wonder whether or not it will or should lead to marriage. We ask ourselves: What is the purpose of marriage? We wonder if, even if we love our marriage partner, we will ever love or desire anyone else. Everywhere we look we see that life changes and evolves; we wonder if romantic love can be an exception.

Let us turn to these and other questions.

Marriage, Divorce, and the Question of Forever

When two people wish to commit themselves to each other, to share their lives, to share their joys and their struggles, and when they wish to make a statement to the world around them about the nature of their relationship, to give it social objectivity, they look to the form or structure of a marriage agreement as a means through which to express, solemnize, and objectify their choice.

The institution of marriage, certainly as it exists today, is a response to our desire for, and perhaps need of, structure. This does not mean that every couple who fall in love automatically think of marriage; many do not. More and more couples currently are choosing to live together without marriage in the legal sense. But if and when they do choose to marry, I think their motive is best understood in terms of a very human, very natural longing for structure.

We can acknowledge the legal and financial considerations that often make marriage desirable, considerations having to do with the protection of children, questions of inheritance, and so forth. These practical considerations can obviously be important. But I do not believe they represent, for most people, the essence of marriage or the ultimate grounds for its existence.

The desire for structure is hardly irrational. It is only irrational to imagine that structure per se will solve all the problems of human relationships. Clearly, it doesn't.

Neither religion nor the state created marriage. They merely arrogated to themselves the right to sanction or bless or otherwise control a relationship that developed out of the choices and needs of individual men and women. This point needs to be stressed because sometimes resentment of religious or political involvement in the marriage agreement turns into resentment against marriage itself. Yet the two issues are entirely separate.

The essence of marriage—especially in the sense we are concerned with here—is not legal but psychological. There are people who live together without legal sanction and yet who are more truly married, psychologically, than others who have participated in a formal wedding ceremony. The essential issue is one of *commitment*.

This means, first of all, the acceptance, without resistance or denial, of the importance of the other person to our life. It means that we experience our partner as essential to our happiness and are at peace with this fact. But it means more than that: it means that our experience of self-interest has expanded to include the interests of the person we love, so that the happiness and well-being of our partner becomes a matter of our personal, selfish concern. Without any denial or loss of individuality, there is the sense of being a unit, especially in regard to the rest of the world. There is the sense of an alliance: Whoever harms my partner harms me. And more: the protection and preservation of the relationship exists on my highest level of priorities, which means that I do not knowingly or deliberately act so as to jeopardize our relationship; profoundly respecting the needs of the relationship, I try to be responsive to those needs to the best of my ability.

It is easy enough to see that if this is the meaning of commitment, most marriages exist with far less than a full measure of commitment on the part of those involved.

Sometimes a couple will ask, "But why bother with all that? Isn't it enough that we love each other? Why marry? Especially since we don't plan to have children." Marriage is not an obligation; it is a choice. No one can reasonably say that two people "should" get married. There is no rule about it. If a couple wish to live together without the formal commitment of marriage, there are no grounds for urging them to change their policy. Marriage is too difficult and hazardous an undertaking to be entered into without total, unreserved enthusiasm. At the same time, it is hard to escape the impression—which some recent studies seem to support—that antipathy to marriage is linked

in the minds of many people with a *fear of commitment,* fear of dedicating themselves totally and unreservedly to *any* relationship.

The ability to make the kind of commitment that
marriage logically requires presupposes a reasonable
level of maturity. It presupposes, among other things,
the wisdom to choose a partner with whom sustaining
such a commitment is realistically possible. We know,
of course, that the younger people are when they
marry, the more likely it is that the marriage will end
in divorce. This is hardly surprising. Unfortunately, the
ideal age for child-bearing is not the ideal age for
marriage, at least as we are now psychologically consti-
tuted. We must live with the fact that the great majority of young marriages will end in divorce, and there is
every reason to believe that the divorce rate will be
even higher in the future. Divorce has become, increasingly, a normal way of life; it is not a *deviation* from
the normal pattern, it *is* the normal pattern.

And yet, most people who divorce remarry subsequently. They may have lost their joy in a particular
partner, but they have not lost their enthusiasm for
marriage, judging by the statistics on second and third
marriages. Marriage continues to represent the preferred state for most men and women.

While lifelong monogamy is still the more-or-less
official ideal of our culture, the social reality seems
better described by a different pattern: *serial* monogamy. We are only married to one person at a time
(monogamy), but in the course of our lifetime we may
be married to two or three people (serial monogamy).

This need not be viewed as a misfortune or a tragedy. There is no necessary implication in this of taking
marriage lightly or irresponsibly. *It is an error to
assume that a marriage is invalid if it does not last
forever.*

The value of marriage is to be gauged by the joy it
affords, not by its longevity. There is nothing admira-

ble about two people remaining together in marriage, thoroughly frustrated and miserable, for fifty years.

Morever, it would be an error to assume that serial marriage is becoming more and more the norm only because of people's immaturity, only because most people do not know how to function effectively in a love relationship or to choose a partner wisely in the first place. Important as this consideration is, it is only one of the reasons marriages end.

We have to recognize that change and growth are of the very essence of life. Two human beings, each pursuing separate paths of development, can encounter each other at a point in time where their wants and needs are congruent and can share their journey over a period of years with great joy and nourishment for both. But a time can come when their paths diverge, where urgent needs and values impel them in different directions, and it can become necessary to say good-bye. This is painful, undeniably; we want to cling, we want to hang on, we sometimes passionately resist the forces within ourselves that urge us into new and unfamiliar situations.

I am thinking of a romance I witnessed between a twenty-two-year-old woman and a forty-one-year-old man. He had recently come out of an unhappy marriage, she out of a highly frustrating relationship with a very immature youth. Looking at the older man, she saw a maturity she had never experienced in a man, combined with an excitement for life that seemed to match her own; looking at her, he saw in her eyes an appreciation of his excitement and a radiant excitement of her own that he had not experienced with his wife. They fell in love; for awhile they were ecstatically happy together. Time passed and frictions slowly and subtly developed between them. She wanted to be free, to play, to experiment—in a word, to be young; he wanted the stability of a firm commitment. Gradually they saw how different were their respective stages of development and, consequently, many of their wants and needs. They felt compelled to say good-bye. But was their relationship a failure? I do not think they would say so. Each one of them gave the other something beautiful, something nourishing and memorable.

Sometimes couples choose to place the preservation of the relationship above other growth or developmental needs and to repress the impulse to move along new pathways. The security and value of what they have takes precedence over the possibility of what they might become. This is a choice. We take what we want—and we pay for it. Sometimes romantic love survives this choice; sometimes it doesn't.

Interlude: Process Versus Structure

It is very common these days to hear such assertions as "Monogamy doesn't work." Or "Marriage doesn't work." There is a sense, of course, in which these statements are true. There is another sense, however, in which they are totally misleading. The fact is nonmonogamy doesn't work, either, and neither does nonmarriage. For most people *nothing* works.

There is certainly no evidence to suggest that being unmarried makes most people happier than being married. The reverse is true. And there is no evidence to suggest that being nonmonogamous makes people happier than being monogamous. Every choice creates its own problems and generates its own difficulties.

When I am asked, do I believe in monogamy (more precisely, in sexual exclusivity) or do I believe in marriage, I cannot answer the question as stated. I neither believe nor disbelieve. There is an inaccurate presupposition in the question.

The implication of the question is that one structural arrangement between people is inherently superior to another, regardless of who the people are, regardless of their psychology, regardless of how they conduct themselves, regardless of how they deal with their partner. I call this the "structure approach" to human relationships. In contrast, I am a proponent of the "process approach." The difference is this: The structure approach puts its primary emphasis on the *form* that a relationship takes; the process approach puts its primary emphasis on what specifically happens between the people involved. When I speak of "the form" of the relationship I refer to such matters as whether or not two people live together, whether or not they are married, whether or not extramarital affairs are an agreed-on part of their understanding, and other matters of this kind. When I speak of "process" I refer to the kinds of behavior that go on between them, the kind of issues discussed in this chapter.

If, to take an extreme example, two couples choose to live together in a "four-person marriage," this is an issue of the *form* of the relationship; it does not yet tell us how the four people will deal with one another, which is a question of *process*. It does not tell us, for example, whether they will own their feelings or deny them, whether they will express their wants or conceal them, whether they will be interested in anyone else's context or only in their own, whether their dealings will be honest or manipulative, whether they will make one another feel visible or invisible, whether they will create an atmosphere of respect and dignity or hysteria and game playing. If the *processes* by which they deal with one another are rational, appropriate, grounded in respect for reality, they will discover soon enough whether or not a four-person marriage works for them. If their processes are *not* rational, *not* appropriate, *not* grounded in reality, *nothing* will work for them, neither a four-person marriage, nor a two-person marriage, nor casual affairs, nor celibacy.

The point is that if a person does not know how to deal sensitively and intelligently with his or her lover, taking a second lover will probably not enhance wisdom. It will merely expand the area of incompetence. And if a person does have the sensitivity and intelligence to deal with another human being in a love relationship, then he or she will know that there are not absolute rules concerning such matters as sexual exclusivity and that such issues are always a matter of the context, individual histories, personal life-styles, developmental and emotional needs, and overall psychology of the persons involved.

In matters such as sexual exclusivity, about which we will talk more shortly, we cannot realistically write prescriptions that will fit the whole human race. Solutions must be custom-tailored to individuals, not acquired "off the rack."

If the old-fashioned orthodoxy was that only sexual exclusivity between partners is moral, appropriate, psychologically healthy, then the new orthodoxy, in some quarters, is that only multiple sexual relationships are moral, appropriate, psychologically healthy. Once upon a time, if a couple came for marriage counseling because one party desired to have an outside affair, the consensus was that the problem belonged to the person desiring the outside affair; today it is often considered to be the problem of the party who objects. I do not believe that this is progress. Both views assume that someone must be guilty, that there is one right pattern for everyone and that whoever is outside the pattern needs to be "fixed."

Whatever choices we make, there will be consequences. Of all proverbs I have ever heard, my favorite is a Spanish one which says, " 'Take what you want,' said God, 'and pay for it.' " Mature people project consequences in advance—and take responsibility for their actions. Sometimes, it is true, we cannot foresee all the consequences of an action; but if we choose to take it anyway, we need to be clear about our uncertainty and about the fact that consequences we may not like will follow.

There are individuals who know how to make marriage and sexual exclusivity work for them. There are individuals (smaller in number) who know how to make nonmarriage and nonsexual exclusivity work for them. In both cases, they are a minority.

I can think of couples who began their relationship on the premise of sexual exclusivity, then later chose to drop that requirement, then later chose to reinstate it. I can think of couples who began their relationship on the premise of nonsexual exclusivity, then later felt the need for it, then once more returned to their first choice. Sometimes such relationships survive; sometimes they don't. " 'Take what you want,' said God, 'and pay for it.' "

If I go by my own experience and the experience of colleagues with whom I have discussed the question, most couples or individuals who have experimented with sexually "open" relationships in their younger years are generally inclined, by the time they are in their forties or early fifties, to favor sexual exclusivity. This seems to be the conclusion of Nena O'Neill, in *The Marriage Premise* (1977), which was written some years after Ms. O'Neill coauthored the famous book, *Open Marriage* (1972). The reasons seem to involve the desire for a firm commitment, the stability and security that result from total dedication to one person and one relationship, plus, no doubt, a certain boredom or disenchantment with the pursuit of sexual variety for its own sake. There is the feeling that romantic love, in the context of an exclusive relationship, may in the end be the most exciting adventure there is.

This is my own conviction.

Sexual Exclusivity

But within the context of marriage or, for that matter, of any romantic relationship where there is serious commitment, what of the question of sexual exclusivity?

When we love passionately, I believe the desire for sexual exclusivity is entirely normal. When we love passionately, the act of sex is experienced by us as anything but "merely a physical act," because it is such a powerful vehicle for our expression of love. It is not only our bodies that meet in bed, it is our souls. In consequence, the thought of our partner sharing that particular response with another person is painful. Cultures that take extramarital sex for granted are not cultures in which marriage is associated with intense passion.

I do not wish to imply, let me say at the outset, that an extramarital affair, if it happens, should or will necessarily lead to catastrophe for the primary relationship. Not at all; I am simply observing that the *desire* for sexual exclusivity is thoroughly understandable and is *not* a manifestation of neurosis or merely a remnant of "old-fashioned conditioning."

At the same time, we are sexual beings and we do not cease to become sexual beings—fortunately—when we fall in love. We do not become blind to the rest of the human race merely because we are in love, although it sometimes seems that way for awhile. We are not oblivious to the attractiveness of human beings other than our partner. Sometimes our awareness of that attractiveness generates desire. Whether or not we will choose to act on the desire is another question entirely, but that such a desire can arise, and almost certainly will from time to time, seems an obvious and inescapable fact of human psychology.

Obviously, the more secure we are within ourselves, the stronger our self-esteem and the stronger our sense that we are loved and desired by our partner, the easier it is for such occasional desires in our partner to be accepted by us. We are not obliged to enjoy them, but neither are we inclined to catastrophize them. On the other hand, if we are insecure within ourselves, if it never really felt plausible that anyone should love us, and if we suffer doubts about the depth of our partner's love and desire for us, then any sexual response of our partner toward another person almost inevitably generates anxiety if not panic. We live waiting for the ax to fall.

Assessing the matter realistically, it seems clear that long-term sexually exclusive relationships are far more likely to happen in the second half of life than in the first. When people fall passionately in love in their forties, they are not so likely to be still sexually in-experienced; there is a better chance that much of their sexual curiosity has been satisfied; and they are more likely to be interested in and psychologically motivated to preserving a sexually exclusive, or at least *pre-dominantly* sexually exclusive, relationship.

When people fall in love and marry in their twenties, the likelihood of their preserving that relationship, with or without sexual exclusivity, across a lifetime, is very remote, as we have already noted. In our twenties we are very unlikely to be sufficiently developed to be able to make a lifelong commitment. And even if our choice of partner is appropriate at the time, even if it is a wise, intelligent, and mature choice, the normal process of change, growth, and evolution may generate differ-ent desires and needs in later years.

To make this point clear, consider that if our normal life expectancy were a thousand years, no one would imagine that a couple marrying in their twenties were marrying "for life." It would be recognized that their commitment was a commitment to share *part* of a journey, not its entirety. And if our life expectancy were five hundred years? A hundred years? Where is the line to be drawn?

None of the foregoing is intended to deny that there are people who marry in their twenties or thirties and do remain together, happily together and with sexual exclusivity, for as long as both of them live. What needs to be challenged, however, is the assumption that any other pattern necessarily represents a fail-ure.

Let us consider some of the reasons persons involved in an important primary relationship may sometimes find themselves drawn to outside sexual encounters. We are *not* discussing relationships in which there is neither serious love nor serious com-mitment.

A common popular assumption—quite mistaken, as it happens—is that the basic reason for extramarital affairs is sexual frustration in the primary relationship.

While this is sometimes the case, it is far from being a universal explanation. Many persons engage in outside relationships with partners they perceive as less attractive and less sexually exciting than their mate. What is involved, often, is a powerful desire for novelty and variety.

Especially when people marry who have had little or no previous sexual experience, it is highly likely that in later years they will wonder what they might have missed, what else might be "out there" that they don't know about, and extramarital experimentation can follow as a consequence.

But at any age, and regardless of our past experience, an outside affair is sometimes sought to relieve what we experience as the staleness of our existence, to relieve a generalized sense of tedium or boredom, or is sought as consolation for some frustration, not in our primary relationship, but in our work or career.

All of these considerations may be subsumed under the concept of the hunger for new stimulation, new levels of excitement. Yet we need to look more closely at this desire for novelty and variety, not because it is not often real and authentic, but because it is an explanation often used to cover a multitude of other motives. In other words, sometimes it is the explanation offered but is not a true explanation. It is unnecessary, in this context, to attempt to list all the possible factors that might lead to an extramarital sexual encounter other than a hunger for novelty, but listed below are some common motives worth recognizing.

Sometimes what is involved is the desire to assure ourselves that we are still attractive; the desire is for ego enhancement or ego gratification.

Sometimes we wish to be with a person who does not know our history, has not seen our growth, is not familiar with our faults—who sees us as a fresh person, as it were.

Sometimes we feel hurt by our partner and an affair is a form of revenge or ego salvaging. Sometimes we are retaliating for an affair undertaken by our mate.

Sometimes we are involved with a partner whose own life scenario *requires* a mate who will be "unfaithful," who will "wrong" him or her, who will "betray" him or her, and we who have the affair may be totally unaware of having been manipulated into it by the "wronged" and "betrayed" partner.

Sometimes extramarital affairs arise simply out of loneliness, as when circumstances cause partners to be separated from each other for some period of time.

Sometimes we meet a new person of a kind who, in our earlier years, we felt we could not possibly have, and now, when the opportunity is presented, the temptation may be felt as irresistible.

Sometimes we meet a new person who strikes chords within our being that have never been struck before; new doors are opened; new understandings and new gratifications are experienced. And we feel drawn to encounter this new person on every level—including the sexual—even though the attachment may not be strong enough to motivate us to separate from our primary partner.

My purpose is not to evaluate these motives as "good" or "bad," but simply to draw attention to them and to the fact that they should not be obscured beneath clichés about the "desire for novelty."

One thing seems clear: It is an error to assume that if two people "really" love each other it is impossible for either of them to have an affair—or to desire one—with anyone else.

Some people are far more comfortable with sexual exclusivity than others. Some people, no matter how much they love, would probably experience several decades of sexual exclusivity as more or less impossible for them. We do not understand all the reasons for these differences in psychology. What is certain, however, is that neither moral applause nor moral condemnation nor swift and easy universal prescriptions are of any value whatever.

We might wish that such problems did not arise in the course of our marriage. We might hope that they will not arise. And indeed they may not. But if they do, wisdom asks that we do not catastrophize, do not conclude that the only possible meaning is that love is gone, do not conclude that our relationship is now unavoidably doomed.

I can think of cases in which an extramarital affair seems to have strengthened the primary relationship. I can also think of cases in which it seems to have destroyed it. One has to look at each situation in its own terms, in its own context.

I do not think anyone can reasonably argue against the fact that extramarital affairs threaten a primary relationship. When we open a door and walk through it, we cannot know for certain what lies beyond. Let us not ignore the obvious: When our partner has affairs with other people, we usually feel hurt, and too great an accumulation of pain can cause love to die. This does not mean that the couple necessarily separate; they may continue, but on different terms; the character of the relationship has changed; their new accommodation may still include love, but they may no longer wish to characterize it as romantic love. The fire is gone.

And yet . . . I am thinking of a couple who had the wisdom to see very clearly that the involvement of one of them in an extramarital affair pointed to some unresolved problems in their relationship. They saw that that was the time not to surrender to fear but to summon their courage and their wisdom, to fight for the relationship, not to abandon it. They saw that their most imperative need was to understand *why* the affair happened. They succeeded, and their relationship was reborn and revitalized.

If our partner sleeps with someone else it is understandable that we may feel hurt or angry. Perhaps we feel frightened; perhaps we feel threatened. But whatever we may feel, we need to understand that no good purpose is achieved by attempting to hold and control our partner by means of guilt, by means of reproaches. The impulse to attack, to lash out, may feel very natural. But if the preservation of romantic love is our purpose, we need to recognize that this is not a strategy that heals, it is a strategy that alienates. Neither is it a healing strategy to pretend an indifference we do not experience. What is needed is not lies, but understanding and an honest effort at communication.

Some couples accept the fact that outside affairs can happen, and agree, in principle, to accept them, providing there is full disclosure. Other couples express a preference for discretion and silence; they agree, in principle, to accept such affairs, but ask not to be told about them. Both policies have their hazards.

Whatever choice and decisions a couple makes will have consequences. Sometimes a couple will begin with one policy, realize it does not work for them and change to another. All one can say, both to those couples who are inclined to sexual exclusivity and to those who are not, is, "Be as honest with each other as you can be about your feelings, preferences, and actions. Don't lie to yourself. Don't lie to your partner. And you'll discover what works for you and what doesn't work for you."

In any event, I am personally convinced that a continuing practice of deception can poison the best of relationships. Lies are unavoidably alienating. Lies create walls, barriers.*

What seems to be changing today, and changing for the good, is an increasing unwillingness on the part of people to live with lies in this area—an increasing impatience with a life of deception, and a greater desire for the whole issue to be brought into the open.

It seems clear that fewer and fewer couples today are willing or able to dedicate themselves to sexual

---

*The difficulty in writing about such a subject is that almost anything one says can be misinterpreted. For example, I have just stressed the desirability of honesty. But there are men and women who, when they have extramarital affairs, run home to tell their spouse in intimate detail what they have done, blow by blow, caress by caress, as if their spouse were a "Mummy" or "Daddy" whose blessing they were seeking. When challenged, they might very well insist that they are merely practicing the virtue of honesty.

exclusivity across a lifetime. Men and women will need the wisdom, early in their relationship, to face this issue squarely, to formulate a policy for dealing with it that each can live with. Ideally, they will formulate a policy *before* the issue arises.

One cautionary observation seems appropriate at this point. A possible pitfall in extramarital relationships, which I have seen again and again, is that they *make marriages bearable.* Hence they may keep the men and women involved from confronting the pain and frustrations in their primary relationship; their affairs are not a solution but an anodyne, a pain-killer. So for those who are tempted by extramarital affairs, it can be very important to ask: How do I imagine I would feel about my marriage if I were *not* to have extramarital affairs?

It is easy enough to declare, dogmatically, that sexual exclusivity is the only workable life-style for everyone, or to declare, equally dogmatically, that "open" sexual relationships are the only practical answer. Neither assertion shows adequate respect for the subtleties and complexities of relationships or the profound differences that exist among people.

There are no easy answers.

Jealousy

This is clearly the appropriate moment to consider the problem of jealousy and romantic love.

The first thing we should understand about *jealousy* is that it is a word used to describe a variety of emotional states that are by no means identical. It is confusing when, for example, the same word is used to describe the simple pain we might feel at learning that our partner has slept with another person, the frenzied suspiciousness of a person who is constantly seeing signs of infidelity where none in fact exist, and the anxiety-ridden possessiveness of a person who cannot bear for his or her partner to find value or pleasure in any other human being, male or female.

In a sexual-romantic context, "jealousy" involves feelings of anxiety, feelings of being threatened, fantasies of rejection or abandonment, and, very often, rage, in response to our partner's real or imagined interest in, or involvement with, another person.

There are those who say that jealousy, however understood, is irrational. This is not a view I share. Emotions are neither rational nor irrational. Human beings can be described as rational or irrational; thought processes can be described as rational or irrational; but emotions simply *are*. One might reasonably be tempted to call jealousy irrational in one context only: when it is experienced in the absence of any objective provocation; when it has no basis in external reality. Even then, of course, if we are to speak literally, what is irrational is not the feeling but the distorted thinking processes that give rise to it.

Sometimes people feel jealous because they have deep self-doubts and insecurities and live with constant anticipations of rejection and abandonment. Sometimes they experience jealousy because they feel ignored or neglected by their partner and now see someone else receiving the very consideration they wanted themselves. Sometimes jealousy arises, in a new relationship, because of painful experiences in past relationships involving the partner's involvements with other people. Sometimes jealousy arises because one person has disowned his or her *own* sexual interest in other people and projected the problem onto the partner. Sometimes jealousy comes out of a generalized apprehension that somehow happiness will be destroyed. Sometimes jealousy is ignited by the anxiety triggered by the direct knowledge that a partner is involved with another person.

Obviously jealousy can be damaging to romantic love. What is needed to counter this danger is the art of managing jealousy when it arises.

Typically, when people are jealous they respond with anger, accusations, tears, and character assassination of their partner. All of this tends to provoke defensiveness and counterattack on the part of the accused party. Screams, denials, lies, or angry silence take the place of authentic communication.

When people feel jealous they very rarely own their feelings honestly. Suppose, for example, that a woman sees her husband flirting with another woman at a party. She is far more likely to become hostile, bitter, or accusing than to say to him, "Watching you, I felt a little anxious, I felt a little scared. I began having fantasies of your running off and leaving me." Were she to speak to him in this manner she would be reaching out in trust; she would not suddenly be treating him as an enemy. She would be taking responsibility for her own feelings. She would have done her part to create a context in which they can talk about the event *as friends*. If her husband does not feel attacked, he does not have to defend. He can listen, he can try to be truthful about his own feelings. If there is a problem, it is one they can face together.

Sometimes, when we honestly admit our feelings of jealousy, when we move from talking about jealousy to the deeper level of talking about anxiety, fantasies of abandonment, and so forth, our painful feelings become less intense or vanish altogether. Each partner needs to learn the art of leaving the surface and going to the root, to feelings of fear, of helplessness, perhaps to memories of past abandonment. If, in the example given above, the husband was attracted to the other woman, it is far kinder to acknowledge this truthfully. If he denies a fact which his wife perceives clearly, he only deepens her anxiety and feelings of distrust. Then, inevitably, her jealousy worsens.

Many a wife has said to me, "It's not that my husband is sometimes turned on to other women that bothers me. I can handle that. It's the fact that he won't admit it, that he always lies about it. That drives me crazy."

One principle is certain here beyond any dispute: If we wish to minimize problems of jealousy in our partner, we must never give our partner grounds to doubt our honesty. And we must never ignore or refuse to deal with our partner's painful feelings.

We always need to go "underneath" the jealousy. If we feel jealous because our partner is sexually interested in, or having an affair with, another person, this principle becomes of extreme importance. We need to go deep into the feeling, deep into the roots of the pain and to experience that, to face it, to talk about it, not to remain on the superficial level of talking about "jealousy." Such talk tends to lead nowhere.

I remember counseling a couple who had been arguing for many months about the husband's feelings of jealousy. All the debates were about whether it was or was not reasonable for him to feel jealous. When he learned to stop talking about jealousy and tell her of his pain, of his fear of losing her, a door opened. She heard him for the first time. She felt loved. She acknowledged her extravagantly flirtatious behavior at parties and cheerfully abandoned it.

Life does not always present us with problems for which there are easy solutions. Our partner may become seriously interested in someone else; we do not know how the story will end, and anxiety and pain may be an inevitable part of what we have to go through. It is very difficult in such situations to be honest about our feelings rather than simply to attack and condemn. Of course, we are not obliged to accept the situation; that, too, is a choice. No one can tell us what we must find acceptable or tolerable. How can there be rules in such matters? Sometimes, when a partner sees how much suffering he or she is causing by having an affair, he or she decides to terminate the affair; but sometimes not. Can we say that he or she "should" or "must" terminate the affair? I do not know who is in the position to make such a statement.

But what if we feel jealousy in the absence of any discernible provocation? What if our partner has done nothing the slightest bit objectionable and still we feel torn by painful suspicions? Of course it is possible that we have received provocation, but of a kind too subtle for the conscious mind to register; at the same time, on the subconscious level, the signal has been received. But there is another possibility that I mentioned earlier: Sometimes, when we deny and disown our own sexual impulses, we attribute them, through the mechanism of projection, to our partner. So a person who is chronically jealous without apparent reason needs to ask: Am *I* interested in outside affairs?

Sometimes jealousy is understood to mean a blow to one's self-esteem or sense of personal worth in response to someone's interest in, or involvement with, another person. By this definition—and it is not without validity—one could say that the more solid one's self-esteem, the less prone one is likely to be to jealousy.

But this may prove to be an overly narrow interpretation of jealousy. What name shall we give to that pain which even the most self-confident people exhibit —or sometimes exhibit—when the person they love becomes sexually involved with someone else? Such pain can be felt without any diminishing of self-esteem.

Let us not ignore an obvious fact: It is, in the nature of reality, possible for our partner to fall in love with someone else. It is a specious notion of maturity to insist that were this to happen, a highly evolved person would be above any feelings of loss. Feelings of loss are painful. We can accept them—we do not have to go crazy or become irrational—but they *are* painful. That is reality.

If either I or my partner feel jealousy—whatever the reasons—and we share our feelings, honestly and openly, without trying to induce guilt, and if the other listens with respect and acceptance and responds with honesty, then we are doing our best to protect our relationship; romantic love may grow. If we deny and disown our true feelings, if we refuse to recognize our underlying anxiety and talk only on a superficial plane; if the other refuses to hear the cry of pain, refuses to respect it, or responds dishonestly, then we are sabotaging our relationship; romantic love may die.

Children and Romantic Love

As we approach the conclusion of our discussion of the challenges of romantic love, it seems in order to say a few words about the subject of children and their impact on a love relationship.

It is clear by now that the vision of romantic love that has emerged in this work goes considerably beyond the concept generally upheld in Western culture. While it has its roots in the Western tradition of individualism and a this-worldly orientation, it is rather a long step away from the ideal of a vine-covered cottage and the patter of little feet—or, to speak more seriously, from the domesticated, "tame" version of romantic love on the one hand and the adolescent fantasy version of romantic love on the other.

Up to this point I have said nothing about the issue of children or the family. This is because my primary focus has been on the psychological dynamics between man and woman. But to ignore the subject completely would surely be to leave a gap in our presentation.

It is true that children can be a beautiful expression of love between two human beings. It is also true that they can be a disaster.

If I focus more on the second possibility than the first, it is because we have all heard so much about the first. We have all heard so much about the gratifications and rewards of raising a family. Those gratifications can be very real. Who can deny the joy of creating a new life and watching it grow? But it is the other side of the story that now needs more attention.

Let us begin with the observation that, as recent studies reveal, many mothers, if given a second chance, would choose not to have children. This is hardly surprising. This fact surfaces in my psychotherapeutic practice very frequently. Of course once children are born we normally become attached to them and love them. This does not alter the fact that, looking back over their life, many women feel, "From what I know today, I see that I could have had a very different life and a more rewarding one had I chosen not to have children."

Across the years I have asked many women, "Do you feel that having children has contributed positively to your marriage, to your relationship with your husband?" The majority of women responded that having children, while rewarding in many ways, was perceived by both them and their husbands as constituting an obstacle to preserving the romance in their marriage. The demands of parenthood are frequently seen not as serving romantic love but as an obstacle that that love needs to overcome.

And yet most women are raised with the view that they are to achieve their destiny through the role of wife and mother. They are educated to define themselves solely in terms of their relationships—to a man and to children. In both cases, "femininity" is associated with "service." And since it is normal to want to be feminine if one is a female, the mystique of motherhood is a very easy trap to fall into—the "bait" is one's self-esteem.

But an interesting paradox is generated: to be "feminine," by this definition, is to place in jeopardy one's ability to function effectively in romantic love.

To state the matter bluntly: The most important thing a woman has to learn in this context is that she has a right to exist. This is the core issue. She has a right to exist and she is responsible for her own life. She is a human being, not a breeding machine whose destiny is to serve others. In other words, women have to learn intelligent and honorable selfishness. There is nothing beautiful or noble about self-annihilation. If romantic love is to be served, to say nothing of individual happiness, this principle must be understood (whether or not one chooses to have children).

A great many women, working with me in therapy,

have confessed that they struggled very hard to persuade themselves that they had "a maternal instinct" in order to feel that they were "truly feminine." Then they go on to acknowledge that after having had three or four children they have to confront the fact that the notion is absurd and has no basis in their own immediate, honest experience.

Let us remember that life consists of making choices. Each one of us has many more potentialities and many more impulses than we are ever going to be able to actualize. Even if there are certain inherent impulses to become a mother, this does not mean that those impulses must be followed. For example, we all probably experience sexual attraction for a great many people across the course of our lifetime. We do not make love to them all. We discriminate. We choose. We evaluate our responses and our inclinations in the light of our long-term goals and interests—or we should. So it is essential to ask ourselves: In the total context of what I want from my life, how will children affect those goals? Am I prepared to give that which the proper raising of children requires?

And, staying with this point a moment longer, if we are concerned with the suppressing of natural impulses, what about all the natural impulses to creativity, achievement, independence, that are commonly suppressed by women who elect to devote their lives to having children?

Further, in considering the impact of children on a man/woman relationship, consider this: Couples are able to take a great many risks, in the interests of advancing their growth and development, that are far more difficult when they have children. For example, one can throw over a boring, unrewarding job and take a chance on some new venture more easily if no one is involved but two adult individuals who are quite capable of taking care of themselves. But with children? The whole situation becomes different. How many great opportunities are passed by, how many chances are not taken, how much growth is stifled because a man or a woman is afraid to make a move that might threaten the well-being of children? And if, because we have allowed too many opportunities to pass us by, our lives feel more and more weighted, more and more colorless, it is foolish to imagine that romantic love will remain unaffected.

Studies clearly indicate that contrary to the popular myth, children do not help a marriage but tend to make it harder for the marriage to proceed happily. The biggest problem confronting a couple who plan to have children is how they will preserve a romantic relationship in the context of assuming the role of mother and father. Studies reveal that friction between couples tends to increase with the birth of the first child and the relationship between the couple begins to improve when the last child leaves home.

Another kind of problem is presented to romantic love when one member of a couple desires to have children and the other does not. Obviously this is an issue that is best resolved before marriage. A psychotherapist friend of mine, when doing premarriage counseling, suggests that a couple planning to get married should fantasize where they see themselves being in five years, how they see their life, and then share their fantasies with each other. Sometimes they discover in this manner that they have very different goals, very different dreams. Care and thought must be given to negotiating those differences; otherwise it is almost inevitable that romantic love will be a casualty.

It is not hard to understand why two people who love each other would want to share the adventure of creating a new human being. I am hardly arguing that no one should have children. My argument is against having children as a matter of routine, or blind social tradition, or out of a sense of duty, or out of the need to prove one's femininity or masculinity. My argument is against having children without awareness of the potential impact on romantic love.

Let me simply say, in conclusion to this discussion, that those men and women are particularly to be admired who, choosing thoughtfully and responsibly to have children, know how to preserve the integrity of their love relationship against the demands of parenthood. To accomplish this is no easy task.

Preserving an Abstract Perspective

The sustaining of romantic love requires two attitudes or policies that superficially may appear contradictory. One is the ability to be in the present, to be in the moment. The other is the ability to hold an abstract perspective on one's life and not get lost in the concretes that may immediately confront us. We realize that this is not a contradiction when we acknowledge that it is necessary both to see the trees *and* the forest.

Sometimes couples fight; sometimes they feel alienated. Sometimes our partner may do something that hurts or exasperates us. Sometimes we—or our partner—want passionately to be alone for awhile. None of this is unusual or abnormal. None of it is inherently a threat to romantic love.

One of the characteristics of mature love is the ability to know that we can love our partner deeply and nonetheless know moments of feeling enraged, bored, alienated, and that the validity and value of our relationship is not to be judged by moment-to-moment, day-to-day, or even week-to-week fluctuations in feeling. There is a *fundamental equanimity,* an equanimity born of the knowledge that we have a history with our partner, we have a context, and we do not drop that context under the pressure of immediate vicissitudes. We remember. We retain the ability to see the whole picture. We do not reduce our partner to his or her last bit of behavior and define him or her solely by means of it.

In contrast, one of the manifestations of immaturity is an inability to tolerate temporary discord, temporary frustration, temporary alienation, and to assume in the face of distressing conflicts or difficulties that the relationship is finished. Some couples seem to decide this several times a month. They have little or no staying power, little or no ability to see past the immediate moment, little or no ability to reach for a broader perspective on their immediate problems. So their life, and their love affair or marriage, hangs always on the edge of an abyss. This is not an environment in which love grows. It is an environment in which, sooner or later, love tends to wear out.

We need the ability to remain in contact with the essence of our relationship in the face of temporary mishaps, conflicts, hurts, or estrangement. We need the ability to see the essence of our partner, past what our partner may be doing at this moment. We need not to step outside the moment but to see the essence of our relationship and our partner *in* the moment, even when the moment is not a happy one.

Then, even our times of struggle can in the end strengthen love.

I recall something beautiful once said to me by a man very much in love with his wife. "No matter how upset she sometimes gets with me—and believe me sometimes her eyes are really blazing—her face always shows that she loves me and that she knows it, even at that moment. I feel very good because the other day she said the same is true of me; she said my eyes always show that I love her, no matter what else I'm feeling."

Clearly this is one of the secrets of self-rejuvenating relationships.

The Final Challenge: The Longing for Permanence and the Inevitability of Change

When men and women embark on a career in their twenties or early thirties that they intend to pursue across a lifetime, they rarely assume that the next forty or fifty years will be one smooth flight from triumph to triumph. If they have any maturity at all, they know there will be high points and low points, unexpected detours, unforeseeable problems and challenges, occasional crises, and days when they will wake up in the morning wondering why they chose this particular career and whether they are really suited for it.

But when men and women embark on that journey called marriage (or any serious relationship), they tend to do so with far less realistic appreciation of the challenges and vicissitudes that await them. The decision to marry is, rationally, the decision to share a journey, to share an adventure, not to lock oneself away in some womblike, unchanging paradise. No such paradise exists.

Love is a necessary condition for happiness in marriage, but, as we have seen, it is far from being a sufficient condition for permanent happiness.

The desire for permanence, especially when we are deeply happy, the desire to hold the moment forever, may be thoroughly understandable; but such an arrangement cannot be had. Not because love is impermanent—love can be the most permanent thing in our life—but because change and motion are the most natural things in this universe.

Someone said that every relationship needs to be redefined roughly every five years. It may be seven or eight years rather than five, but the principle is correct.

Just as a human being does not remain immutable, but evolves through stages of development, so do relationships. And in each case, different stages have their own challenges and their own distinctive gratifications. When a new relationship is forming there is the excitement and stimulation of novelty; there is also the anxiety of not knowing whether or not the relationship will grow and prevail. Later, with greater security and stability, there is some loss of the excitement and novelty; there is the serenity of problems solved, of understanding achieved, and the joy of discovering that *harmony contains its own excitement*.

Sometimes, especially when problems that need to

be faced and solved arise in a relationship, there is a turning away from the present and a longing for the past, a yearning for what cannot possibly recur. A man dreams of the days when his wife was content just to love him, just to be there for him; why has she suddenly decided that she wishes to resume her education? What has happened to the young girl he married? Instead of welcoming this process of growth, instead of seeing that he too must continue to grow, he fights the process, he resists, he makes himself the enemy of his wife's evolution. Whether he crushes her spirit and ambition and she gives in or whether he drives her away by his lack of respect for her needs, the love is destroyed, the marriage is destroyed.

Sometimes a couple break up, not because their growth and development require it, as they may tell themselves, but because one of them fought and resisted the process of the other's evolution. One of them tried to freeze a moment that had already vanished. One of them lacked the flexibility and inner security to allow the emerging change to happen, to flow with it, to learn what new possibilities might open for both of them.

A man may have held the same job for fifteen years; suddenly or not so suddenly he is dissatisfied, he is bored, he feels unfulfilled—he wants a new challenge. His wife is bewildered and frightened. What will happen? Will they be as financially secure as they were in the past? Why is he losing interest in their friends? Why has he taken to reading so much? Is he going to become interested in other women next? She panics. When he tries to explain his feelings, she does not listen. She is terrified of losing what she has. And out of her terror she proceeds to lose it.

A husband complains that his wife is scatterbrained, that she cannot even balance her checkbook. He loves her, he says, but how he wishes she were more mature! Something happens; through some mysterious process of growth he had not noticed, she becomes more responsible. She takes an interest in his business. She asks intelligent questions. She decides to start a business of her own. He is devastated; what has happened to the wonderful little girl he was so happy with? She looks into his eyes and sees an enemy, the enemy of her self-realization. She wants his love, she wants their marriage, but she wants to be a human being too. Shall she revert to being a little girl again—and hate her husband for the rest of her life? Shall she continue to fight for her own development—and drive her husband away?

These are the kind of hard and painful choices that many a couple has to face.

Every relationship has a system. And in a system when one part or component changes, the other parts and components must change also—or else equilibrium is lost. If one partner grows and the other partner resists growth, disequilibrium arises, then a crisis—then a resolution, or a divorce, or worse than a divorce: a long, slow process of disintegration made of dying love, bewildered anguish, and hatred.

If we have the self-confidence and the wisdom to be the friend of our partner's growth, then that growth need not be a danger or a threat. But if we set ourselves against it, we only invite tragedy.

And by the same token, if we attempt to protect our relationship by aborting our own growth and evolution, again we invite tragedy. We deprive our self and our relationship of *aliveness*.

Life is motion. Not to move forward is to move backward. Life remains life only so long as it advances. If I am not evolving, I am decaying. If my relationship is not getting better, it is getting worse. If my partner and I are not growing together, we are dying together.

But stillness is impossible. The moment can be lived, but it cannot be captured. We must be in the moment, feel it, experience it, then let go, then move on—to the next moment and the next adventure. And we cannot demand always to know in advance what that will be.

It is obvious that the attitude I am proposing requires self-esteem. Here again we can see the importance of self-esteem to the success of romantic love. It is self-esteem that gives us the courage not to fight change, not to fight growth, not to fight the next moment of our existence. *And the exercise of that courage in turn strengthens our self-esteem.*

Our greatest chance at permanence lies in our ability to handle change. Love has the greatest chance to endure when it does not fight the flow of life but learns to join with it.

If my partner and I feel that we are truly the friends of each other's growth, then that is one more bond between us, one more force to support and strengthen our love. If my partner and I feel that, out of fear or bewilderment, we make ourselves the enemy of each other's growth, then that is but a short step from feeling that each is the enemy of the other's *self*.

I am thinking of a woman I know who is afraid of any change in her and her husband's life that she does not initiate. When she was a child, her father abandoned her mother for another woman, and somewhere deep within her there is still abandonment anxiety. So when her husband, in his fifties, proposed certain changes in the direction of his career, she very subtly talked him out of it without ever opposing him directly. She got her way. But I saw something within him die. Neither she nor her husband may ever recognize the chain of cause and effect, but in one form or another she will pay for her "victory." I wish that she could have owned her anxiety, talked about it openly and honestly, and at the same time been a better friend to her husband's dreams.

To understand and respect our longing for permanence, and at the same time to ally ourselves with the process of growth and inevitable change—this may be the ultimate challenge of romantic love.

If we do have the wisdom and courage to be the friend of our partner's dreams and aspirations, then we have the very best chance that our love will indeed be "forever."

Epilogue: A Final Word on Love

I do not know if there has ever been a time in history when the word *love* has been used quite so promiscuously as it is at present.

We are told constantly that we must "love" everyone. Leaders of movements declare that they "love" followers they have never met. Enthusiasts of personal-growth workshops and encounter-group weekends emerge from such experiences announcing that they "love" all people, everywhere.

Just as a currency, through the process of becoming more and more inflated, has less and less purchasing power, so words, through an analogous process of inflation, through being used less and less discriminately, are progressively emptied of meaning.

It is possible to feel benevolence and goodwill toward human beings one does not know or does not know very well. It is not possible to feel love. Aristotle made this observation twenty-five hundred years ago and we still need to remember it. In forgetting it, all we accomplish is the destruction of the concept of love.

Love by its very nature entails a process of selection, of discrimination. Love is our response to that which represents our highest values. Love is a response to distinctive characteristics possessed by some beings, but not by all. Otherwise, what would be the tribute of love?

If love between adults does not imply admiration, if

it does not imply an appreciation of traits and qualities that the recipient of love possesses, what meaning or significance would love have and why would anyone consider it desirable?

What are we to think, then, of such a statement as the following, made by Erich Fromm (1955): "In essence, all human beings are identical. We are all part of One; we are One. This being so, it should not make any difference whom we love."

If we were to ask our lover why he or she cared for us, consider what our reaction would be if told, "Why shouldn't I love you? All human beings are identical. Therefore, it doesn't make any difference whom I love. So it might as well be you."

Not everyone condemns sexual promiscuity, but I have never heard of anyone who hails it as an outstanding virtue. But *spiritual* promiscuity? Is *that* an outstanding virtue? Why? Is the spirit so much less important than the body?*

The kindest thing one can say about current uses of "love" is that such usages represent inexcusable intellectual sloppiness. My own impression is that people who talk of "loving" everyone, are, in fact, expressing the wish or plea that everyone should love them. But to take love—above all love between adults—*seriously,* to treat the concept with respect, and to distinguish it from generalized benevolence or goodwill, is to appreciate that it is a unique experience possible between some people but not between all.

When a man and woman with significant spiritual and psychological affinities encounter each other and fall in love, if they have evolved beyond the level of problems and difficulties described in this study, if they are beyond the level of merely struggling to make their relationship "work," then romantic love becomes the pathway not only to sexual and emotional happiness

---

*Commenting on this paradox, Rand (1957) writes, "A morality that professes the belief that the values of the spirit are more precious than matter, a morality that teaches you to scorn a whore who gives her body indiscriminately to all men—the same morality demands that you surrender your soul to promiscuous love for all comers."

but also to the higher reaches of human growth. It becomes the context for a continuing encounter with the self, through the process of interaction with another self. *Two consciousnesses, each dedicated to personal evolution, can provide an extraordinary stimulus and challenge to the other. Then ecstasy can become a way of life.*

It is this vision of the possibilities of love that has animated the writing of this book.

One day Devers—the woman I am in love with—said to me, "What you are writing is a love story." At first I thought she meant Patrecia. But then I realized that she meant something else entirely. What this book is about is my own love for love, my love for the experience and adventure that love offers. And in that sense Devers is right: This is a love story.

Devers and I were married a few weeks ago, as I was approaching the completion of this chapter. A new journey begins.

Bibliography

Aristotle. Nicomachean Ethics. *The Basic Works of Aristotle.* Trans. W. D. Ross. New York: Oxford University Press, 1940.

Bossard, James H. S., and Eleanor S. Boll. *Why Marriages Go Wrong.* New York: Ronald Press Co., 1958.

Branden, Nathaniel. *The Psychology of Self-Esteem.* New York: Bantam Books, 1971.

————.*The Disowned Self.* New York: Bantam Books, 1973.

Burgess, Ernest W., and Harvey T. Locke. *The Family: From Institution to Companionship.* 2d ed. New York: American Book Co., 1953.

Cuber, John F., and Peggy B. Harroff. *The Significant Americans.* New York: Appleton-Century-Crofts, 1965.

de Rougemont, Denis. *Love in the Western World.* Rev. ed. Trans. Montgomery Belgion. New York: Pantheon Books, 1956.

Friday, Nancy. *My Mother/Myself.* New York: Delacourt Press, 1977.

Fromm, Erich. *The Art of Loving.* New York: Harper and Brothers, 1955.

Ginott, Haim. *Teacher and Child.* New York: Macmillan Publishing Co., 1972.

Greenfield, Sidney M. Love: Some Reflections by a Social Anthropologist. *Symposium on Love.* Ed.

Mary Ellen Curtin. New York: Behavioral Publications, 1973.

Hazo, Robert G. *The Idea of Love*. New York: Frederick A. Praeger, 1967.

Hoffer, Eric. *The True Believer*. New York: Harper and Brothers, 1951.

Hunt, Morton. *The Natural History of Love*. London: Hutchinson and Co., 1960.

Janus, Sam, Barbara Bess, and Carol Saltus. *A Sexual Profile of Men in Power*. Englewood Cliffs, N.J.: Prentice-Hall, 1977.

Koestler, Arthur. *Janus*. New York: Random House, 1978.

Langdon-Davies, John. *A Short History of Women*. New York: Literary Guild of America, 1927.

Linton, Ralph. *The Study of Man*. New York: D. Appleton-Century Co., 1936.

Mahler, Pine, and Bergman. *The Psychological Birth of the Human Infant*. New York: Basic Books, 1975.

Maslow, Abraham H. *The Farther Reaches of Human Nature*. New York: Viking Press, 1971.

Masters and Johnson. *The Pleasure Bond*. Boston: Little, Brown and Co., 1970.

Mead, Margaret. *Coming of Age in Samoa*. New York: New American Library, 1949.

Murstein, Bernard I. *Love, Sex, and Marriage Through the Ages*. New York: Springer Publishing Co., 1974.

O'Neill, Nena. *The Marriage Premise*. Philadelphia: M. Evans and Co., 1977.

Peele, Stanton, with Archie Brodsky. *Love and Addiction*. New York: New American Library, 1975.

Praz, Mario. *The Romantic Agony*. Trans. Angus Davidson. 2d ed. London and New York: Oxford University Press, 1951.

Rand, Ayn. *Atlas Shrugged*. New York: Random House, 1957.

————. *For the New Intellectual.* New York: Random House, 1961.

Schneider, Isidor, ed. Marriage and Sex Love. *Origin of the Family in the World of Love.* Vol 2. New York: George Braziller, 1964.

Taylor, G. Rattray. *Sex in History.* New York: Harper Torchbooks, 1973.

von Bertalanffy, Ludwig. *Problems of Life.* New York: Harper Torchbooks, 1960.

————. *Organismic Psychology and Systems Theory.* Barre, Mass.: Clark University Press, Barre Publishers, 1968.

Index

We Deliver!
And So Do These Bestsellers.

SPECIAL
MONEY SAVING
OFFER

Now you can have an up-to-date listing of Bantam's hundreds of titles plus take advantage of our unique and exciting bonus book offer. A special offer which gives you the opportunity to purchase a Bantam book for only 50¢. Here's how!

By ordering any five books at the regular price per order, you can also choose any other single book listed (up to a $4.95 value) for just 50¢. Some restrictions do apply, but for further details why not send for Bantam's listing of titles today!

Just send us your name and address plus 50¢ to defray the postage and handling costs.

BANTAM BOOKS, INC.
Dept. FC, 414 East Golf Road, Des Plaines, Ill 60016

Mr./Mrs./Miss/Ms. _____
               (please print)

Address _____

City_____ State_____ Zip_____

FC—3/84